JANCOVICI - BLAIN

WORLD WITHOUT END

PARTICULAR BOOKS

an imprint of

PENGUIN BOOKS

PROLOGUE

August, 2018. My partner and I are bound for the Breton shore in our little rental.

It must be pushing 25°C.

There's a heat wave in Paris.

Look! According to this article, temperatures in Paris and eastern France will reach 50°C by 2050.

It's an interview with paleoclimatologist Jean Jouzel, a former member of the IPCC (Intergovernmental Panel on Climate Change).

2018 was the first year that a heat wave was linked to global warming all over the mainstream press.

50°C by 2050

It won't happen all at once in 30 years.

How high in 2040?

How high in 2030?

How high in 2020?

We're there!

I'd been hearing about global warming for a while now, but I took refuge in how far away it seemed. Now it was getting real.

Very, very soon after that...

Dear Sir...

Er... nah.

Hello, um...

Uh... Mr. Jancovici...

Uh... I'd like to meet with you... In order to... Er...

Just spit it out!

I get the feeling he's not one for fawning or formalities.

The next day...

Hey!

He said he'll see me!

The day of our appointment, it's scorching. I'm running late...

I asked to meet up in a café. It's got red velvet curtains. It looks like a brothel. I'm a bit ashamed.

Hello.

Sorry!

Uh...

This was the only quiet place with AC in the neighborhood.

The carbon footprint's probably godawful, but at least... we're cool? Heh...

No problem, I was busy working.

Just who is Jean-Marc Jancovici?

I know a little about him now...

...because I'm writing this prologue.

Which means the book is done.

We've been working together for 2 years.

5

Where are you from, Jean-Marc?

In '86, I'd just gotten my degree, and I met an actor who wanted to start a company doing short corporate films...

For an engineering grad from a top school, this was like busking. I made zero money. The others moved on to big companies like Arcelor, Rhône-Poulenc, SNCF, EDF, etc.

It didn't work out. But I stayed in related fields, with ambitions that, by and large, met with success.

While working as an independent consultant with France Telecom in the mid-90s, I came across studies on the development of telecommuting, e-learning...

...the virtual work economy, and thus a reduction in GREENHOUSE GASES...

Greenhouse gases?

What're those?

Back then, not many people were interested in any of this.

I started doing some research...

GREENHOUSE GASES AND GLOBAL WARMING

Until then, I'd never felt a deep interest in any particular subject.

But I was riveted.

There's nothing else for me now.

This is what I want to do when I grow up.

The rest has fallen by the wayside.

In the early 2000s, I developed a protocol for an agency of the Ministry of the Environment. It was called the CARBON INVENTORY.

It gave rise to the global standard for measuring corporate greenhouse gas emissions.

I brought in scientists from different fields: paleoclimatologists, including Jean Jouzel; atmospheric chemists; oceanographers...

At the same time, I was writing articles on global warming in a small magazine for Polytech alumni...

Then I launched my own website, and, in 2002, published my first book, *L'Avenir climatique* ("The Future of Climate").

I became a science popularizer.

Now, we can stuff ourselves, and pay the price...

...or go on a diet.

My career in committees began. I was asked to join an environmental watchdog.

It was a surprise. I hadn't been looking into the topic for long. I was there from 2001 to 2009.

In 2007, I founded Carbone 4 with a partner.

So you're the guy behind carbon accounting? That's crazy! You patented a process used worldwide?

No, the government agency that commissioned the work owns the rights.

It's not like I did it for the money. It's being used... That's the important thing.

We've built a world that tends to bring lots of people together in a single place.

As a system, it requires increasingly colossal influx and outflux to keep going.

When the normal circulation of any flux is impeded, the system breaks down. For example, the flux of humans...

...due to a virus.

Another kind of flux has helped shape this system. Namely...

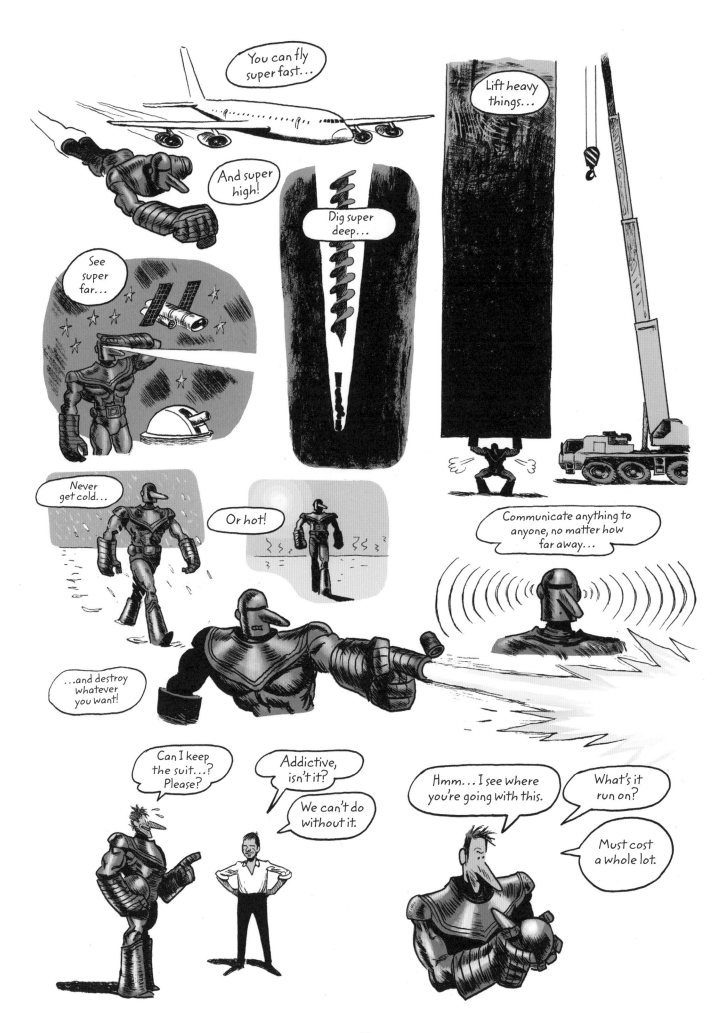

The electricity that is consumed in Manhattan represents 2% of the city's annual revenues.

If you took it away...

I don't think the price per square foot would remain the same...

57 flights up...

The way we rationalize our energy usage makes about as much sense as saying:

Your brain is only 2% of your body weight.

Remove half of it? No biggie— we're only talking 1%!

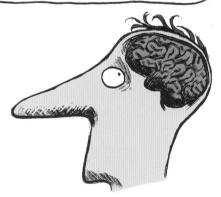

Um...

But wait! Marvel's Iron Man figures out a way to keep his blue energy from polluting.

Couldn't we make something like a renewable Armor Man?

Three hundred years ago, all energy was renewable.

Sailing was 100% renewable.

Blargh!

But we switched to coal-fired ships, and then to gasoline because it gets us our clothes from Vietnam faster...

Blargh!

We had 100% renewable road transportation.

BEEP ♪
BEEP ♪

But when it came to getting oranges from Florida to Chicago, gasoline still proved more efficient.

HONK ♪

We had 100% renewable agriculture. People were eating potatoes and onions and had the breath to prove it.

But if you want steak at every meal, 100% fossil fuel agriculture is better.

We had public works that were 100% renewable. It took two hundred years to build the Notre-Dame in Paris.

Thanks to fossil fuels, it takes one year to build a modern skyscraper.

Our industries were 100% renewable.

The heck am I doing here?

But we realized that was never going to get us a smartphone for $20 a month.

The heck am I doing here?

We've spent the last 200 years replacing renewable energies with fossil fuels.

So, either we're morons... which is up for debate.

Or there are deep-seated physical reasons.

But... how about this example: I love exercising. So I figure maybe I can pedal during the daytime to produce electricity.

Like in *Soylent Green.*

In *Soylent Green* (Richard Fleischer, 1973), the world of 2022 is overpopulated. Food and resources are scarce. The heat is stifling because of the greenhouse effect. Sol (Edward G. Robinson) pedals an old bicycle in a cramped apartment to produce a little electricity and get some light.

Charlton Heston

E.G. Robinson

Yeah! Like that, but better.

Picture a system with pulleys and flywheels that would multiply my strength.

HAHAHAHA!

No way!

You've imported energy from outside. That's the burger you had for lunch!

It was used to operate your legs, which transmitted their energy to your machine.

Your legs can only produce so much energy. Their capacity is limited unless you add motorized assistance...

In other words, *an external energy source.*

But once they start spinning, the wheels go faster than my legs.

You'll spend more time and energy getting your system going. In the end, it won't provide more than the muscle power you originally put in.

Well, shit!

Hahaha! That's the LAW OF CONSERVATION! Told you it'd make you sweat!

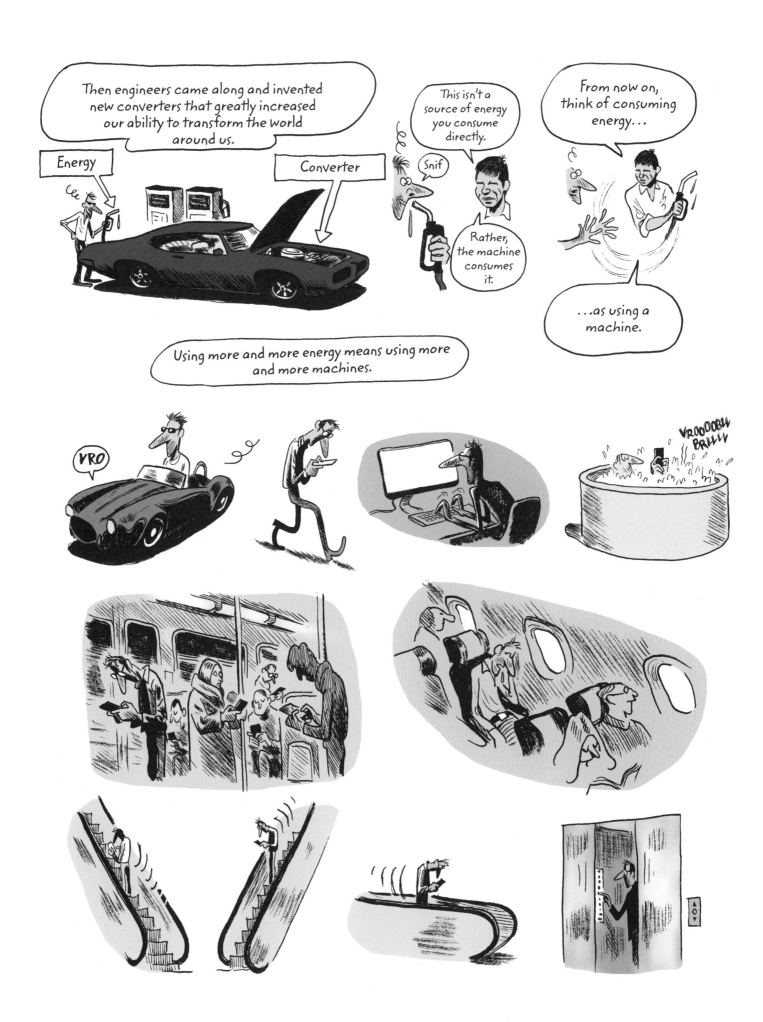

Brush your teeth morning and night?

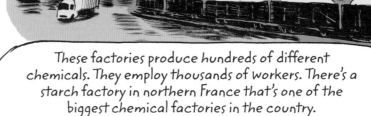

You used a chemical factory, which makes a flavor-enhancing sugar alcohol that doesn't give you cavities so your toothpaste will taste good. This substance is called SORBITOL, and comes from a starch factory that sees full trainloads of corn brought in every day.

These factories produce hundreds of different chemicals. They employ thousands of workers. There's a starch factory in northern France that's one of the biggest chemical factories in the country.

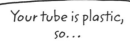

Your tube is plastic, so...

An oil platform again!

Refinery...

Steam cracker...

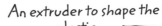

KOF KOF!

Got it, thanks.

An extruder to shape the plastic.

Hm...

So tell me, how is energy measured?

I don't even know what a "kilowatt" is.

In fact, we use "joules."

It takes about 1 joule for 100 g to go up 1 m.

Lifting a chocolate bar one meter represents 1 joule of energy.

Roughly, yes.

Now, burning a liter of gasoline releases about 36,000,000 joules.

That's a lot of zeroes.

Which is why we use kilowatt-hours (kWh).

The combustion of your liter of gasoline makes 10 kWh.

This is *thermal* energy.

With your liter of gasoline, you can power a 10 kW machine for 1 hour.

Or a 100 W machine for 100 hours.

10 kW generator, for example

Power is defined as the energy per unit of time you need.

It is the transformation of the world per unit of time. The more powerful the machine, the less time it takes to transform the world.

The more powerful the heater, the less time it takes to heat the room.

Its *power* is in kW

The *thermal energy* supplied is in kWh

The more powerful the car, the less time it takes to change speed.

Its *power* is in kW

The *mechanical energy* supplied is in kWh

Now you're about to see why machines are so powerful compared to the human body.

Take a 10-kg backpack and climb up to an elevation of 2,000 m.

later

Do you know how many kWh your legs produced during the day?

A bunch.

Nope.

0.5 kWh.

Now for some digging. Excavate 15 tons of dirt, or about 6 m³.

Well?

You've generated 0.05 kWh.

A worker can produce between 10 and 100 kwh of mechanical energy per year.

But 1 liter of gasoline...

At an exorbitant 1.50€...

Burn it, and you'll get 10 kWh of thermal energy.

Run it through a motor, and you'll get 3 to 4 kWh of mechanical energy.

All this to say that just a liter of gas yields the same capacity to transform the environment as 10 to 100 days of hard work from a human.

This energy is incredibly cheap compared to the gain it brings...

If you're getting minimum wage just to use your muscles, the person paying you to transform the environment and carry your 10-kg bag to 2,000 m spent 200€ per kWh.

A machine running on gas would've cost 500 times less.

When you dig, transforming the environment costs 2,000€ per kWh.

And the gas in a machine that makes the same hole costs you 5,000 times less...

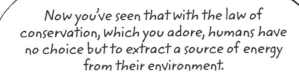
Now you've seen that with the law of conservation, which you adore, humans have no choice but to extract a source of energy from their environment.

Yup!

You've also seen that energy quantifies the transformation of this environment.

Yes.

Well, there is no green energy.

Really?!

Nor pink, nor black.

Nor clean nor dirty, for that matter.

Choosing an energy source means choosing a type of transformation with pros and quid pro quos...

All energy becomes dirty if you use it on a large scale...

Absolutely all.

Look closely at clean energy, and you'll realize it's an energy source used in reduced quantities so as to minimize its drawbacks.

I am extremely clean.

Looking at it the other way around, if humanity used 10 barrels of oil and 1 ton of coal per year, it wouldn't be a problem.

10 barrels is not a lot. Especially since I'm all alone.

I can get a little more.

It won't hurt!

The minute you use an energy source in a massive way, no matter how it is extracted from the environment, there are drawbacks. Choosing an energy source means arbitrating between the acceptable and undesirable drawbacks.

...when it's windy.

When there's no wind, the system comes to a complete halt.

No light, no cold beer waiting in the fridge.

If you don't want the system to stop, add on the price of storage. Batteries, for instance.

That multiplies the cost of the kWh by at least 3, even 4.

Which results in "wind kWh" available on demand at 15 cents or more.

The cost of an oil kWh—which comes pre-stored, since it's already storeable when you take it out of the desert...

...is 0.3 cents.

The price of a kWh from a diffuse, low-density source—the air—is about 100 times more expensive compared to the kWh from a Saudi oil well.

And you still need oil... coal...and gas—to manufacture the wind turbine.

Friendly competition?

C'mon!

Hah!

Whoa!

Where ya runnin' off to, Mr. Windy?

Hm?

Forget your little fossil friend? Did you think you could get along without me?

Remember this:

10 W

100 W

Here's an example of converters from ancient times:

100 W

100 W maximum

1 kW max

It was immoral, and not very efficient, but totally renewable.

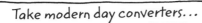

Take modern day converters...

An ordinary tractor

60 kW = 600 pairs of legs, or a few dozen draught animals

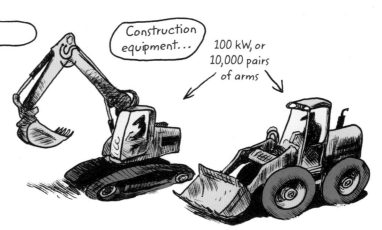

Construction equipment...

100 kW, or 10,000 pairs of arms

These have enabled farmers to increase their productivity a few hundredfold and build a house for the price of a few years' salary.

Which was unthinkable two centuries ago.

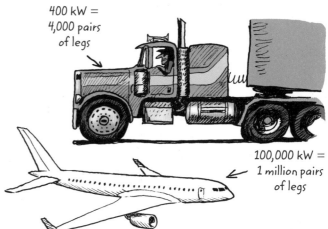

400 kW = 4,000 pairs of legs

100,000 kW = 1 million pairs of legs

An industrial rolling mill...

100 MW = 10 million pairs of arms

That's the entire population of New York City hammering steel.

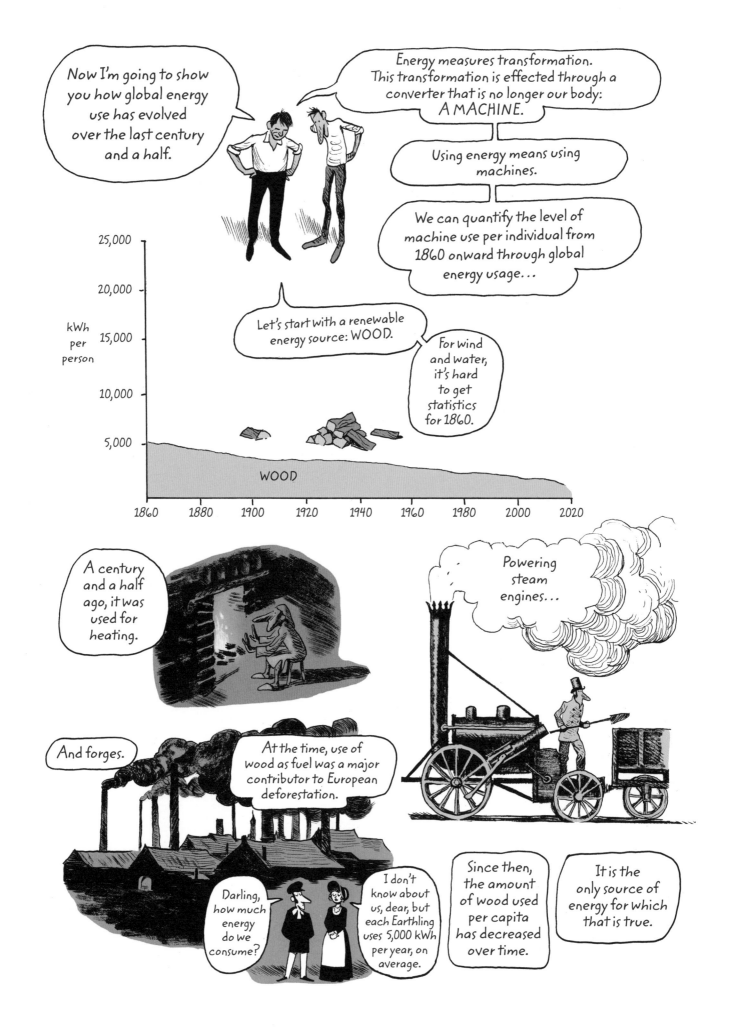

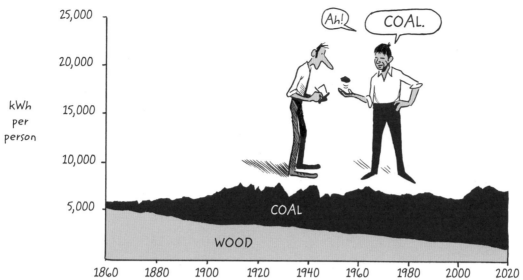

Ah!

COAL.

kWh per person

25,000

20,000

15,000

10,000

5,000

COAL

WOOD

1860 1880 1900 1920 1940 1960 1980 2000 2020

At first we used wood charcoal, then hard coal for forges and the first steam engines.

Coal has always powered steam engines. A power plant is, above all, a large steam engine. Today, 2/3 of coal goes to power plants. About 10-15% is used for metallurgy. The rest is used for heating and industry.

You might not know it, but you use a lot of coal.

You use products imported from countries that use a lot of coal...

Starting with China.

Like your phone!

On average, people use 5,000 kWh of coal per year.

Annual per capita use hasn't gone down since we started using it.

Coal is not a thing of the past.

But it *is* the energy that produces the most carbon dioxide per kWh.

I am carbon dioxide, the primary greenhouse gas produced by human activity.

I'm not absolutely, positively convinced we can do it.

The world's coal-fired power plants put out almost 10 times the power of American electric power plants.

To limit global warming to 2°C (the goal of the Paris Climate Accords), every last one of these coal-fired power plants must be shut down by 2050.

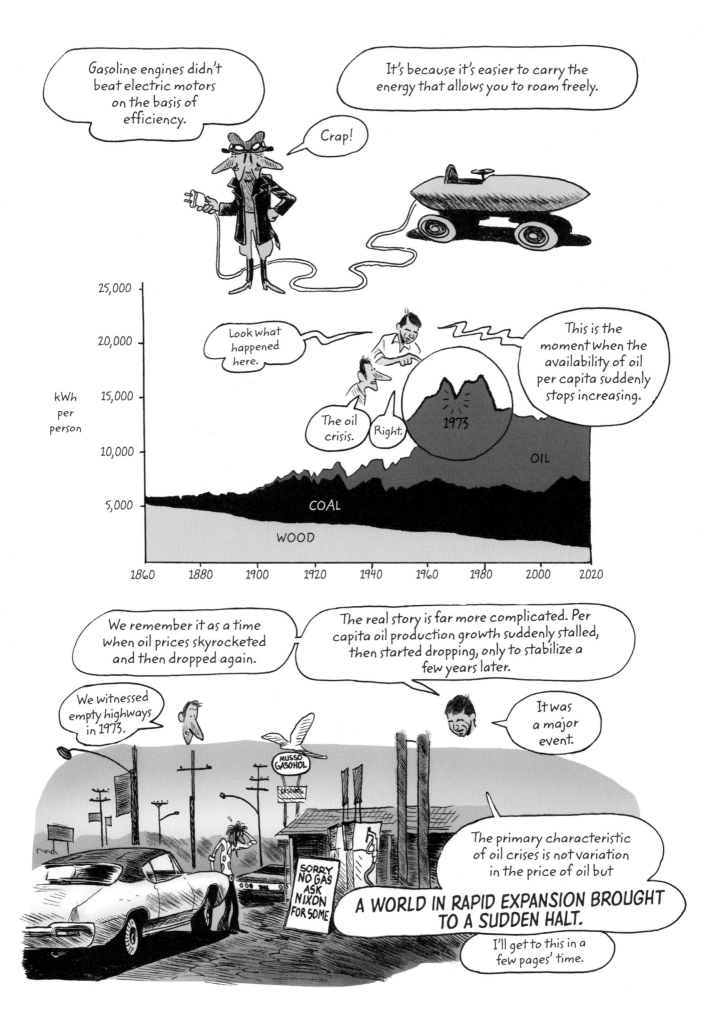

Based on the figures I gave you earlier, it's as if each person on Earth had roughly 200 slaves working for them all the time.

Uh...

Without machines, 1.6 trillion people would have to work to produce the same amount of energy.

...I don't think the Earth can afford to feed 1.6 trillion people.

Instead of eating spinach to get super-strong, we chug a barrel of oil and our exoskeletons become superpowered.

snif
snif

OIL

The machinery that works for us is a kind of exoskeleton. It affords us a mechanical strength that multiplies our muscle power by a factor of 200.

This kind of growing exoskeleton made us into beings with real-life superpowers.

We spend our days using bits and pieces of this suit, like prostheses.

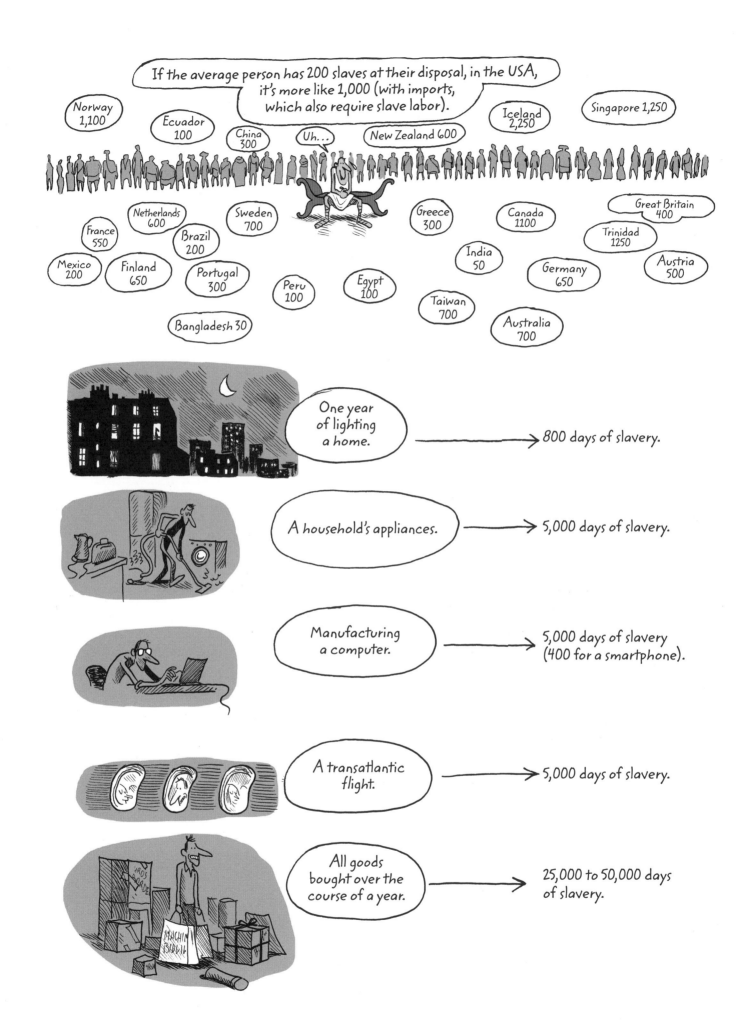

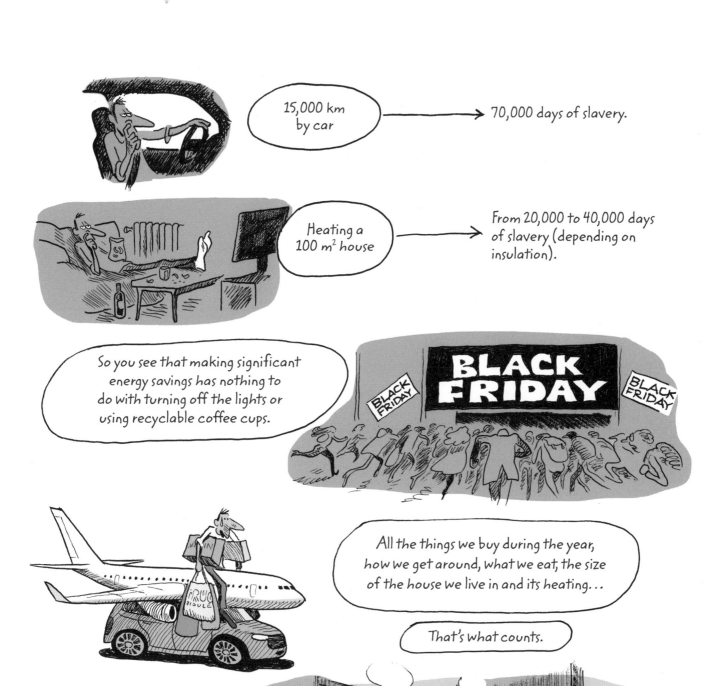

15,000 km by car → 70,000 days of slavery.

Heating a 100 m² house → From 20,000 to 40,000 days of slavery (depending on insulation).

So you see that making significant energy savings has nothing to do with turning off the lights or using recyclable coffee cups.

BLACK FRIDAY

All the things we buy during the year, how we get around, what we eat, the size of the house we live in and its heating...

That's what counts.

This new problem has caught many a company unawares. Their responses have been unscientific, haphazard at best.

Theirs is a world I know well. Addressing the underlying problem would be so... unwieldy. We prefer to look the other way.

We're only human.

We have beehives on our rooftops, and our plastic cups are recyclable!

Plus, we have an annual cycle-to-work day!

47

Per capita energy consumption has increased massively.

But the population has also increased massively.

Humans began to turn away from hunting and gathering 10,000 years ago, as they emerged from an ice age into a warmer interglacial period, an interlude of greater climate stability.

Humans could afford to settle down because the resources they looked to for nourishment no longer roamed at the whim of a changing climate. Culture thus became possible. At the time, humans numbered in the low millions. (Back then, the census wasn't what it is today.)

At the dawn of the Industrial Revolution, circa 1800, the average lifespan was just under 30 years and even shorter in cities, which were rife with germs. Diseases spread more easily there, and the infant mortality rate was higher.

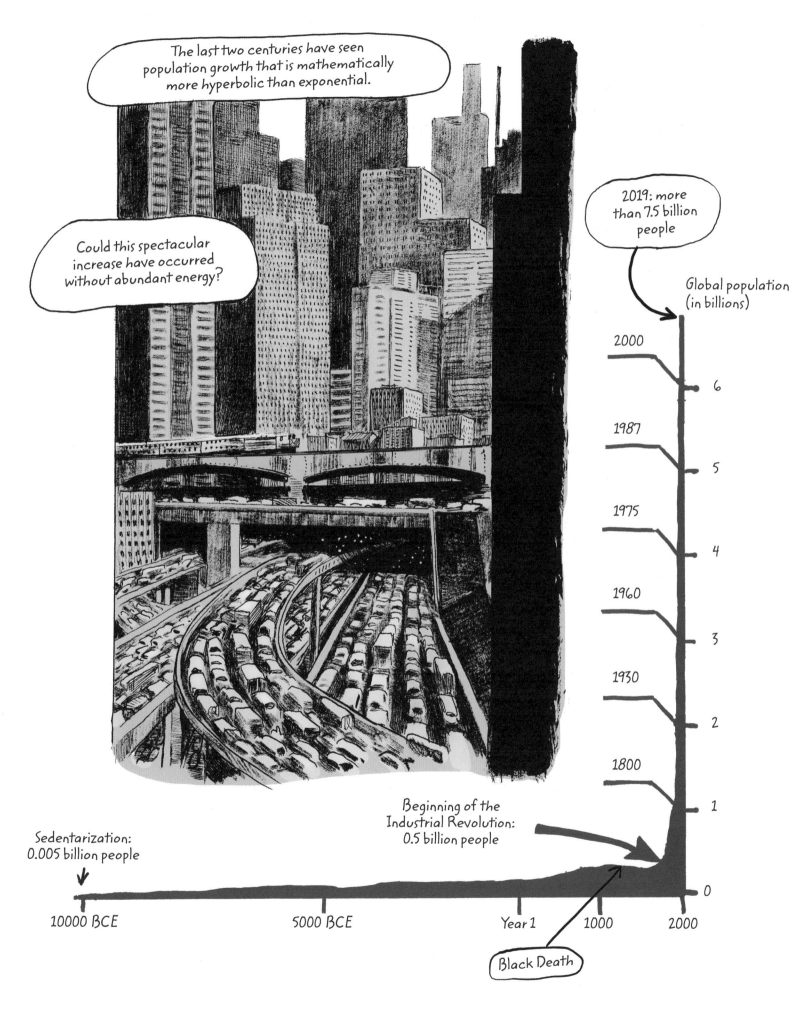

Without abundant energy resources, it's no sure thing that grain yields would have gone from 1,000 to 8,000 kg per hectare in the Paris region between 1935 and today.

Nor is it a sure thing that food could have been transported to places other than where it grew.

It's not entirely certain we could have protected it from the heat, the cold, and all the wee critters wanting to gobble it all up before we do.

It's no sure bet that we could have brought drinkable water to cities and rid them of their noxious fumes...

A fair number of things might not have happened were it not for fossil fuels. Least of all the population of our planet hitting 8 billion...

A population of this size is the result of abundant energy. If we enter a major energy decline, will there still be 8 billion of us?

That's no sure thing either.

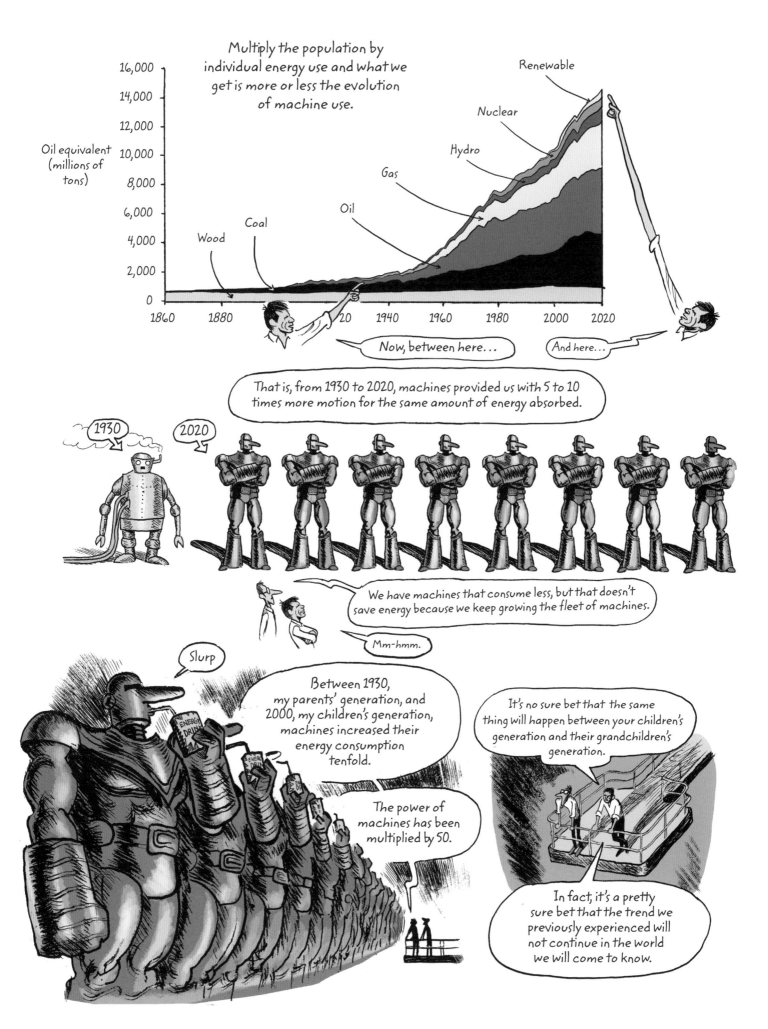

Multiply the population by individual energy use and what we get is more or less the evolution of machine use.

Oil equivalent (millions of tons)

16,000
14,000
12,000
10,000
8,000
6,000
4,000
2,000
0

1860   1880   ·20   1940   1960   1980   2000   2020

Renewable
Nuclear
Hydro
Gas
Oil
Coal
Wood

Now, between here...

And here...

That is, from 1930 to 2020, machines provided us with 5 to 10 times more motion for the same amount of energy absorbed.

1930

2020

We have machines that consume less, but that doesn't save energy because we keep growing the fleet of machines.

Mm-hmm.

Slurp

Between 1930, my parents' generation, and 2000, my children's generation, machines increased their energy consumption tenfold.

The power of machines has been multiplied by 50.

It's no sure bet that the same thing will happen between your children's generation and their grandchildren's generation.

In fact, it's a pretty sure bet that the trend we previously experienced will not continue in the world we will come to know.

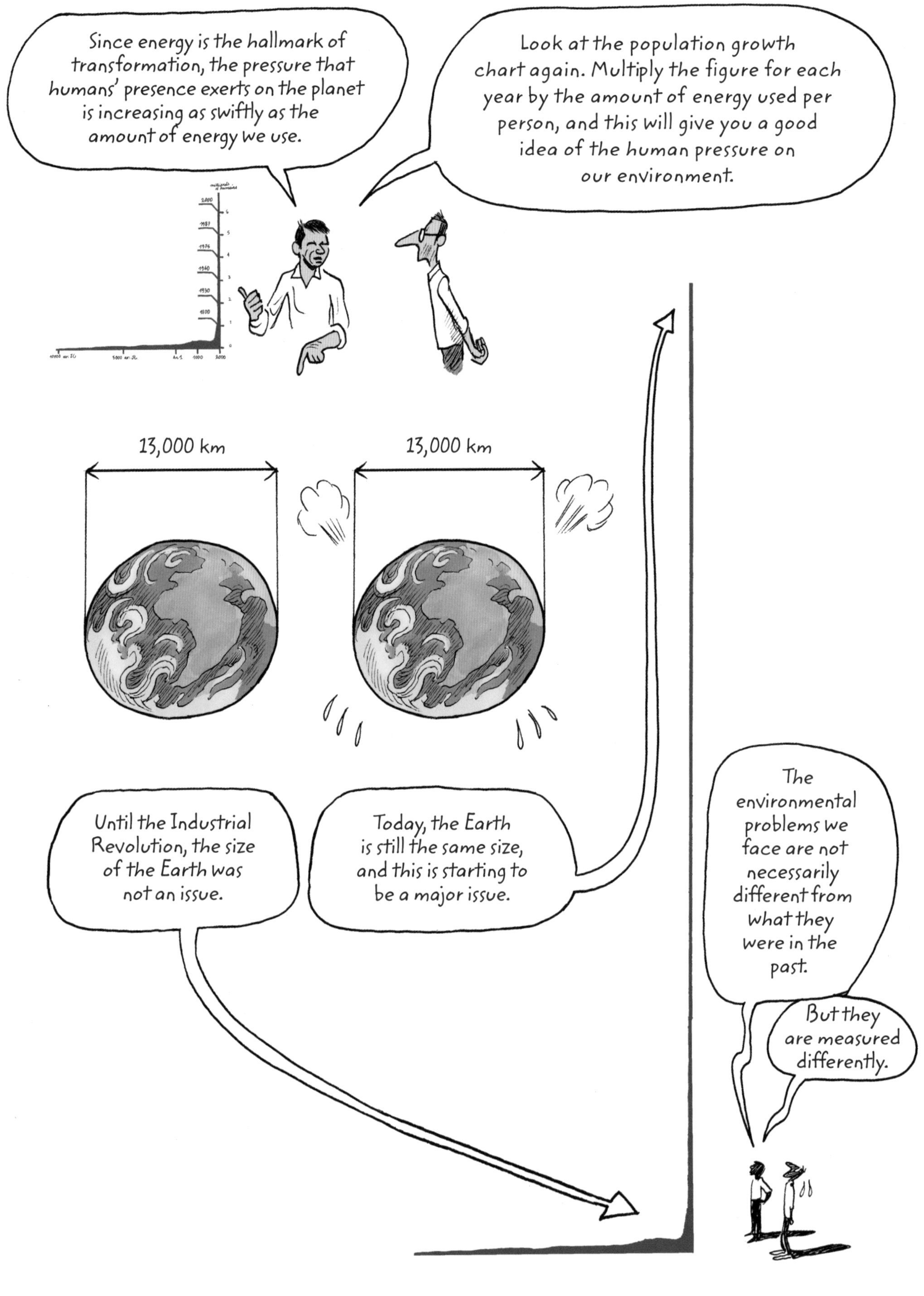

Since energy is the hallmark of transformation, the pressure that humans' presence exerts on the planet is increasing as swiftly as the amount of energy we use.

Look at the population growth chart again. Multiply the figure for each year by the amount of energy used per person, and this will give you a good idea of the human pressure on our environment.

13,000 km

13,000 km

Until the Industrial Revolution, the size of the Earth was not an issue.

Today, the Earth is still the same size, and this is starting to be a major issue.

The environmental problems we face are not necessarily different from what they were in the past.

But they are measured differently.

IN THE PAST

TODAY

The true price of things is not expressed in money, but in minutes of work. You have to correlate the current price with what people earn.

Per capita GDP in the US since 1860 in 1990 dollars:

1860
$2,000

1900
$4,000

1950
$11,000

2000
$27,000

Earnings have increased by a factor of 15, a trend found in all major industrialized countries.

When you look at it this way, the real price of energy has fallen sharply, not because the price of oil has fallen, but because the economic value of work has increased.

The price of a barrel of oil—which has remained relatively stable in constant currency—has dropped by 93% in relation to the population's income.

In the US, the portion of people's income that is spent on energy has been at a historic low during these last 30 years.

Why is it that you can draw instead of working in the fields? Energy abundance.

In general, it has radically changed the world of work.

Almost everyone you know works in the city, in the "tertiary" or service sector of the economy.

This is a new development.

Two centuries ago, 80% of the population worked in the fields.

1821
There were 2.5 million farmers in the US.

In terms of productivity, that means a farmer can feed himself and one third of another person who does something else.

The agricultural workforce increased until 1910. A farmer's productivity didn't change, but the population grew.

These days, we're still cutting down forests to increase agricultural land. This is what happens in all countries with growing populations, until everything that can be cut has been cut.

Then, in the nineteenth century, industry—the first forges—began to develop tools that made farmers more productive.

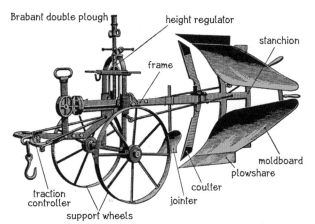

This allows them to reduce the number of workers in the fields, replacing them with draught animals.

But after WWII, Armor Man takes to the fields... for real!

With tractors as powerful as dozens of horses.

But also fertilizers and pesticides...

...which require even more energy than tractors.

Energy abundance enables the use of ever more machines.

This is when industry booms!

A working machine needs someone to run it.

What is a worker's job? Why, to serve a machine.

Before mechanization, tools were an extension of the human. With mechanization, it is the opposite.

Humans once dictated the pace of the tool.

The opposite is true of machines.

	1850	1900	1960	1970
People working in agriculture	55%	40%	8%	4%
People working in industry	15%	20%	23%	28%

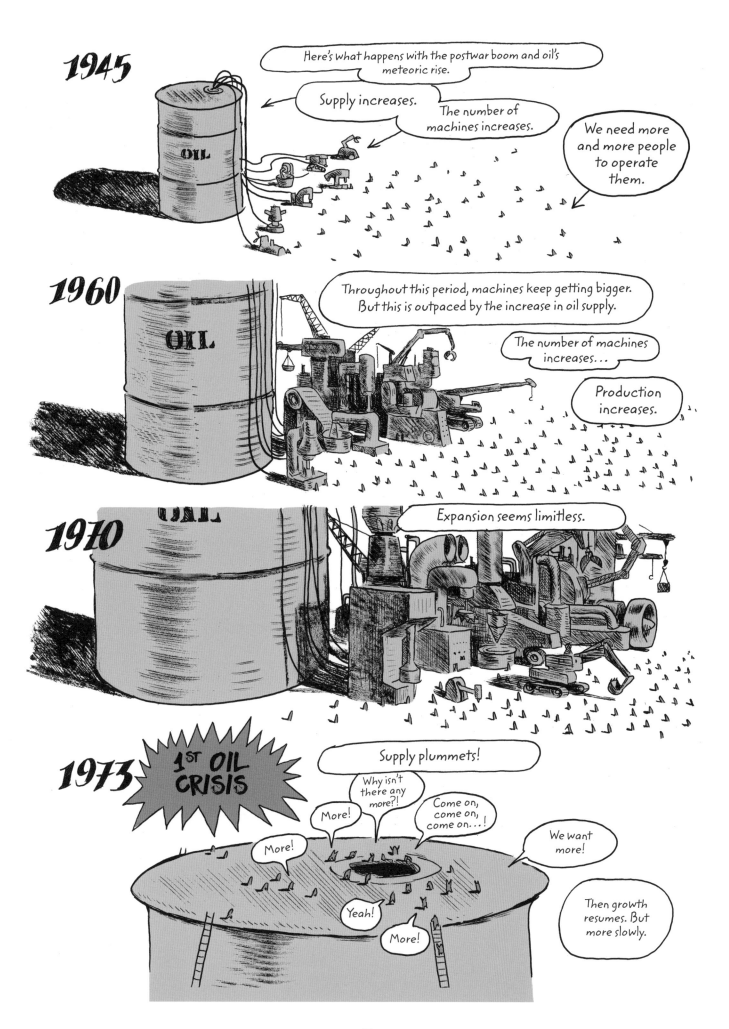

After the oil crises, oil production doesn't increase as rapidly.

Because of this constraint on our energy supply, we can no longer increase both the size and number of machines.

We opt for robotization and automation. Machines grow in size but dwindle in number. Fewer people are needed to operate them.

This doesn't prevent production from increasing.

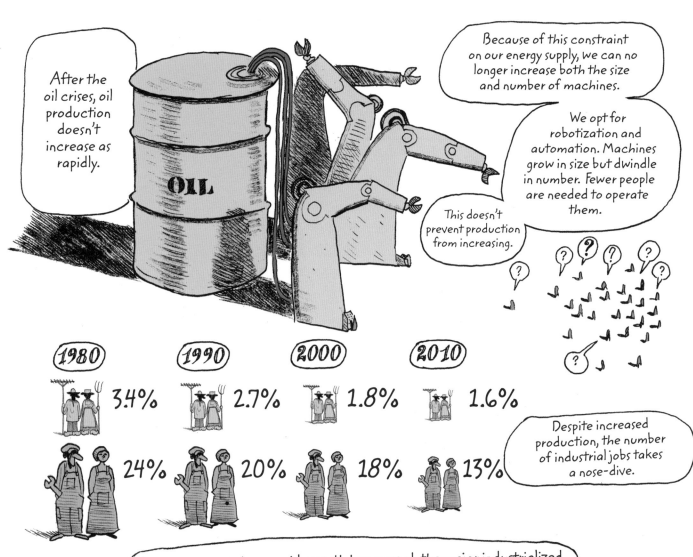

1980	1990	2000	2010
3.4%	2.7%	1.8%	1.6%
24%	20%	18%	13%

Despite increased production, the number of industrial jobs takes a nose-dive.

In an economy where rapid growth has ceased, the major industrialized countries are no longer able to provide high-productivity jobs for everyone.

Some people who can no longer find work in industry go into the service sector...

Unemployment rears its head in the West...

...as do low-skilled, poorly paid, part-time jobs in countries with more liberal systems (Great Britain, the United States, Germany, etc.).

But that's not big enough to absorb this newly jobless population.

JOB CENTRE

Despite everything I've just said, one category of employment positively explodes with the arrival of abundant energy: SERVICE JOBS, THE TERTIARY SECTOR.

In production, the number of machines determines the number of jobs.

In the service sector, jobs are determined by the number of objects produced.

Take cars, for example. More and more cars are produced faster and faster...

But the time it takes to learn to drive hasn't really changed.

Nor the time it takes to sell them...

Nor the time it takes to approve a loan to buy the car...

Nor the time it takes to insure it.

More and more people were needed to manage the distribution of these cars.

Not to mention the jobs that keep erratic drivers in check, for instance.

Service jobs serve the underlying production flow.

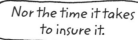

Double production and you double the number of jobs needed to sell, insure, and manage the result.

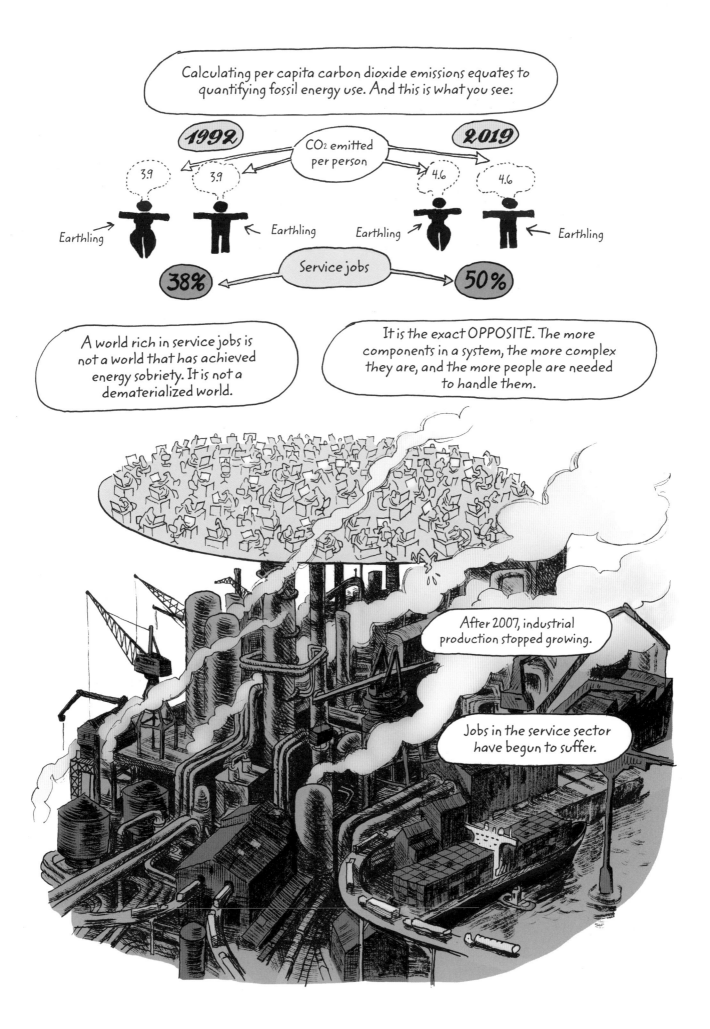

Calculating per capita carbon dioxide emissions equates to quantifying fossil energy use. And this is what you see:

1992   CO₂ emitted per person   2019

3.9   3.9   4.6   4.6

Earthling   Earthling   Earthling   Earthling

Service jobs

38%   50%

A world rich in service jobs is not a world that has achieved energy sobriety. It is not a dematerialized world.

It is the exact OPPOSITE. The more components in a system, the more complex they are, and the more people are needed to handle them.

After 2007, industrial production stopped growing.

Jobs in the service sector have begun to suffer.

The more energy you have available per person, the more machines you have, the less people you have working in agriculture. You see this absolutely everywhere in the world.

Energy abundance has also changed the way we eat.

Historically, we consumed grains and onions...

Then we shifted to small animals. First what they produced...

And then came the French king Henri IV...

I wish no peasant in my realm so poor that he cannot put a chicken in his pot on Sundays.

The hen became a waste product: she spent all her life laying eggs, and when at last she grew too old, we ate her.

Next, we started eating broilers.

Then we started eating pigs.

And finally we started eating cows.

The act of raising cows for consumption is the hallmark of a country dependent on energy as a lifeline. The archetype here is the USA.

Thanks to the productivity that machines have brought about, our ever meatier diets cost ever less.

1929

1971

2013

Portion of income American households spend on food.

20%

Raw products: 80% of the total

10%

5%

Raw products: less than 20% of total

Just over a century ago, households spent 1/4 of their earnings on food. It was like running a restaurant at home.

Today, 80% of our food purchases are mass-distributed.

We used to buy raw products...

...often right from the farmer.

The bulk of your spending does not go toward food.

Cashier's salary

Warehouse worker's salary

Carrier's salary

Engineer's salary from the company that made the automatic payment terminals

Shareholder income

Trucking costs

Advertising revenue

Etc... Anyway, it goes to everything BUT food. Best case scenario, 30% of the price goes to the food itself; worst case, 3%.

A hundred years ago, when we talked about food, there wasn't much processing or middlemen. It's not like that today. What you're paying for are services.

The more processed the food, the more that applies.

The real price of food has been reduced by over 90%, and even more for some items (chicken, chocolate, prawns).

In 1800, a person in Europe consumed an average of 20 kg of meat per year... Today it's roughly 100kg.

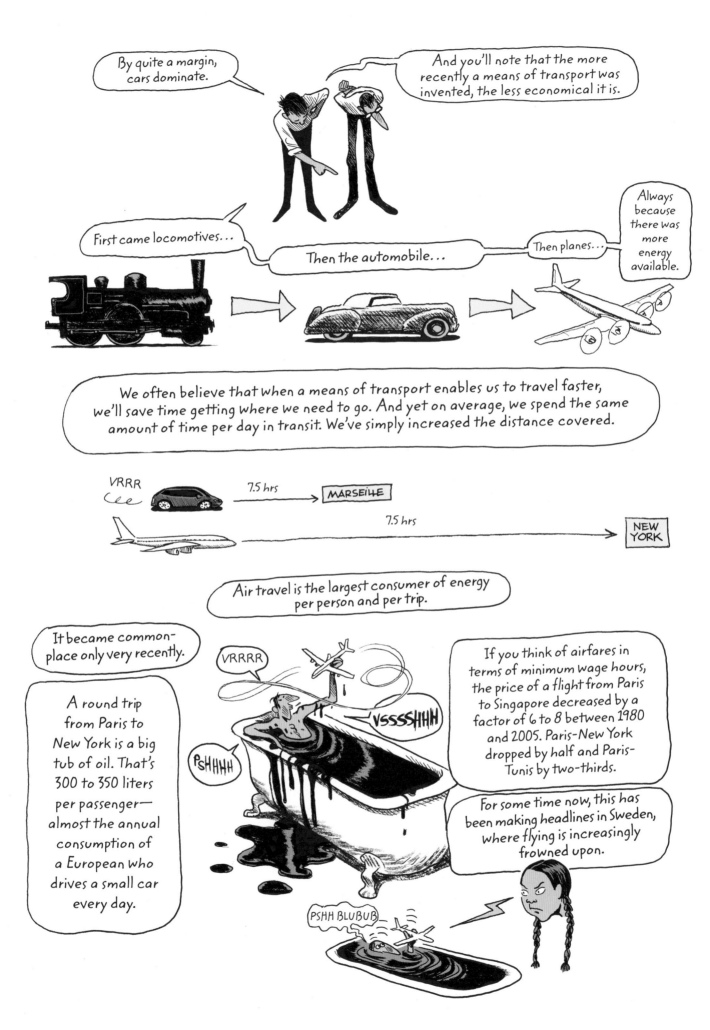

By quite a margin, cars dominate.

And you'll note that the more recently a means of transport was invented, the less economical it is.

First came locomotives...

Then the automobile...

Then planes...

Always because there was more energy available.

We often believe that when a means of transport enables us to travel faster, we'll save time getting where we need to go. And yet on average, we spend the same amount of time per day in transit. We've simply increased the distance covered.

VRRR

7.5 hrs → MARSEILLE

7.5 hrs → NEW YORK

Air travel is the largest consumer of energy per person and per trip.

It became common-place only very recently.

VRRRR

VSSSSHHH

PSHHHH

A round trip from Paris to New York is a big tub of oil. That's 300 to 350 liters per passenger—almost the annual consumption of a European who drives a small car every day.

If you think of airfares in terms of minimum wage hours, the price of a flight from Paris to Singapore decreased by a factor of 6 to 8 between 1980 and 2005. Paris-New York dropped by half and Paris-Tunis by two-thirds.

For some time now, this has been making headlines in Sweden, where flying is increasingly frowned upon.

PSHH BLUBUB

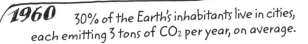

1960 30% of the Earth's inhabitants live in cities, each emitting 3 tons of CO_2 per year, on average.

2014 55% of the world's inhabitants live in cities, each emitting 5 tons of CO_2 per year, on average.

Contrary to popular belief, the more people there are in cities, the more per capita energy usage rises, and the higher the CO_2 emissions.

With its Haussmannian architecture and high population density, Paris offers a prime example of an energy-efficient city. Its buildings are all stuck together.

If you want big towers, you have to leave more space around them.

If you don't have an abundant source of energy, you can do everything on foot (or by horse and cart).

If you give everyone a car, the city sprawls out and becomes LOS ANGELES.

Urban sprawl is a feature of all industrial countries. Cities that haven't given into sprawl have simply met physical barriers.

The urban area maintains the same functions of exchange within a far larger diameter: 90 miles.

Today, the cities that spend least energy on transport are those that are most densely built up.

SINGAPORE

The cities that spend the most are those that sprawl out, Los Angeles being the prime example...

LOS ANGELES

Energy abundance has also enabled the number of dwellings—as well as their size—to increase faster than the population itself.

1973

551 sq. ft per person

2015

1,058 sq. ft per person

This made divorce a lot easier. A divorced couple takes up twice the housing, twice the appliances, and twice the furniture.

This is one of the primary reasons for the increase in housing demand.

If there are children, there are added trips from one home to the other. Separation increases the energy consumption per ex-spouse by 60%.

Machines do work for us. Which frees up our...

TIME

Back when energy was not abundant, advanced degrees were rare, and there was no retirement...

No time for vacations or weekends, no flexible hours...

Take a Boston family

Before 1950

No vacations.

After 1950

A weekend of camping.

300 kg CO_2

When energy is abundant and travel cheap...

A romantic trip for 2 to Paris.

2.5 tons CO_2

A week skiing for 4 in Maine.

1 ton CO_2

A cruise for 2 in the Caribbean.

19 tons CO_2

WELCOME TO Fabulous LAS VEGAS NEVADA

A trip for 4 to Las Vegas.

4 tons CO_2

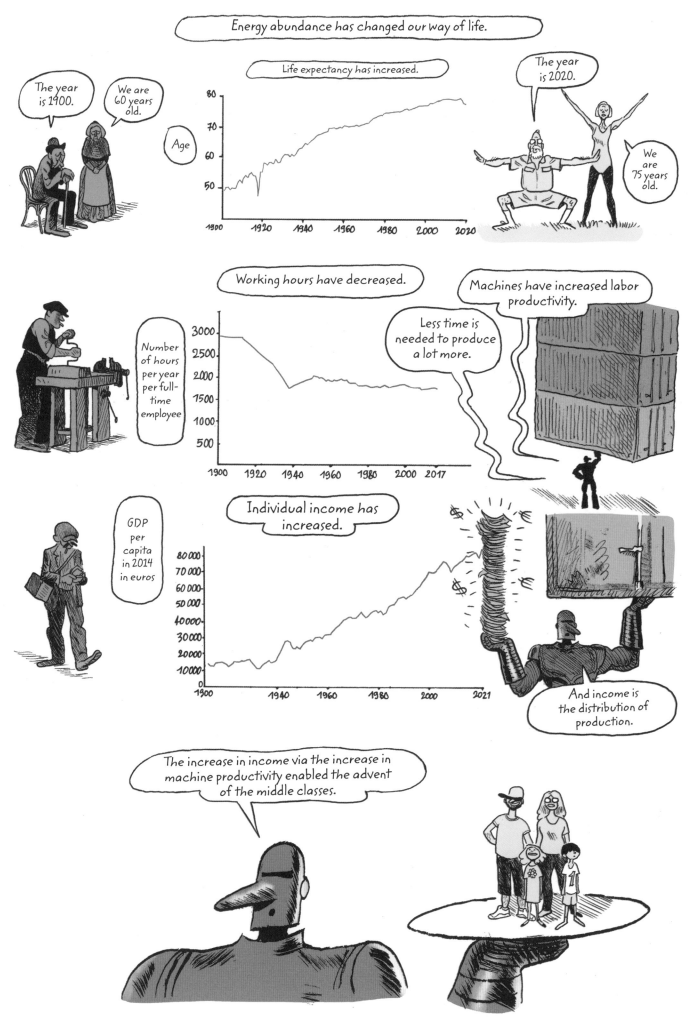

More and more energy abundance has made it possible to produce more and more goods...

Increasing energy abundance has given rise to an increasing flow of information.

Information flows do not replace the flow of goods. The virtual does not replace the physical. The more goods you have flowing, the more information you have and vice versa. Historically, this has always been the case.

Carbon dioxide emissions from digital technology are equivalent to those from...

...the world's entire fleet of trucks!

Or twice the world's commercial ships.

Or 2/3 of the world's passenger cars and commercial vehicles.

Or all of the emissions from American industry.

Even hospitals are energy-intensive. They account for 8% of the US's carbon footprint...

Look around you! Systems that let us tend to chronic and serious pathologies well into our later years exist only in countries with an abundant supply of energy.

Imagine a shrinking world...

Crap! You mean, we might have trouble getting medical care when we're old?!

We act as if the idea of the world shrinking is inconceivable.

The implicit promise was that everyone would have a desk job. Hence a society of machines, an energy-intensive society.

In the old world, before energy abundance and machines, working people were not productive enough to sustain both themselves and a significant fraction of the non-working population.

Families cared for their elderly members on their own.

Only the wealthy went on vacation.

Those ostracized from society were forced to work. They became slaves, galley slaves, convicts.

But there were struggles too.

Yes, but those struggles only really led to a gain in comfort for society as a whole once abundant energy entered the picture.

They aren't only the result of our desire to do something good.

In the postwar boom, when the supply of energy, especially fossil fuels, exploded, all Western nations set up a welfare state, more or less. Less welfare in the United States, more welfare in the Scandinavian countries and France.

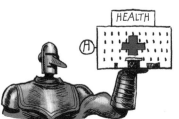

The era's economists deemed that what was scarce, and therefore truly valuable, was human labor.

I concern myself solely with limitations deriving from men.

Who cares about the rest?

Our resources are infinite.

Who cares, I say!

Our economic thinking still works this way.

Resources are infinite...

Yes, who cares!

This is all that interests us.

The French engineer and economist Charles Dupin (1784-1873) conducted another study in 1801:

He compared the French and English forces of productivity.

Shhhhh!

He established rules of equivalence between animals, machines, and men at work.

He understood why Great Britain, with roughly the same population as France, produced almost three times as much.

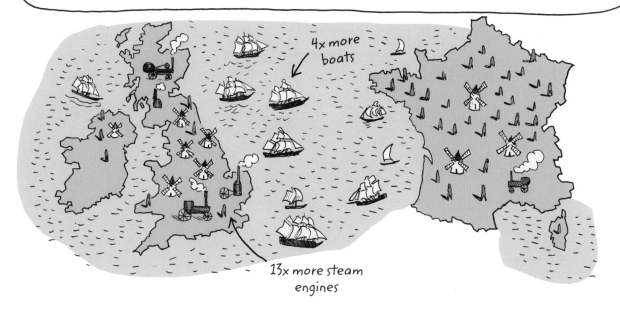

4x more boats

13x more steam engines

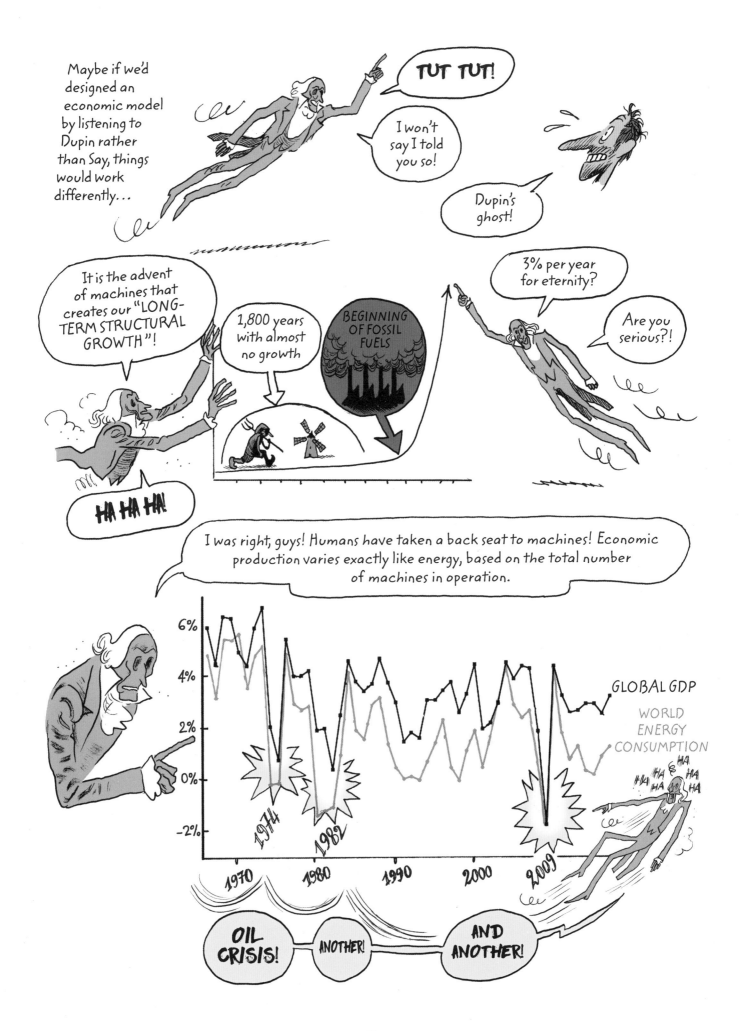

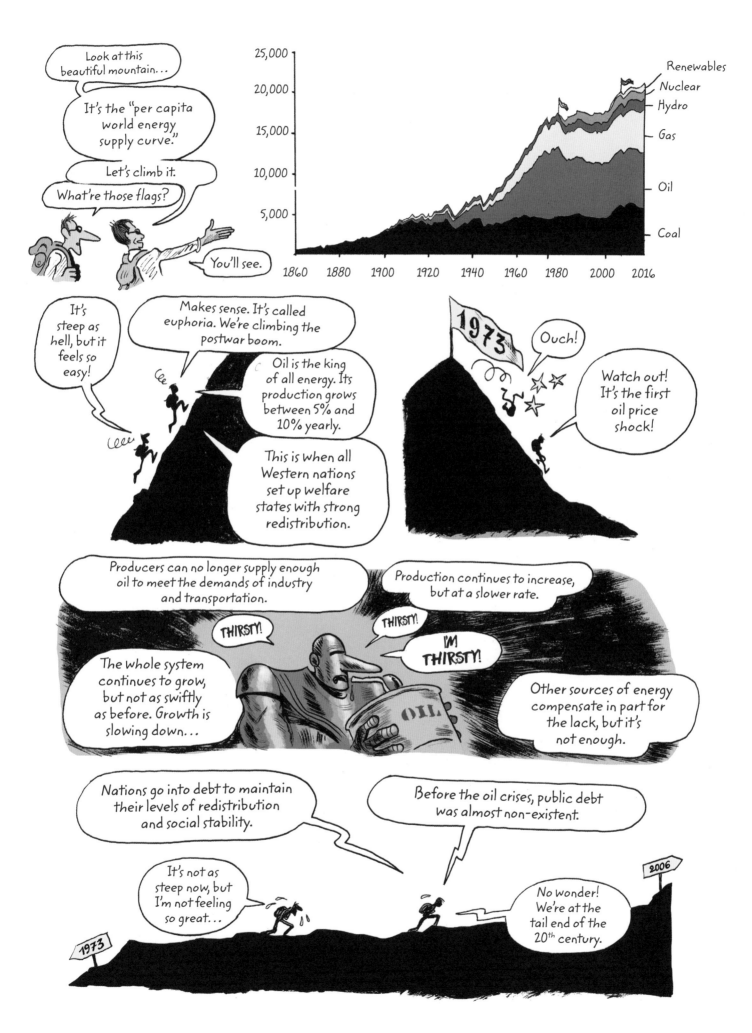

Oil is a fossil fuel. Like all fossils, it is a remnant of ancient life.

Long ago, plankton lived in oceans, some of which no longer exist.

A fraction of these micro-organisms fell to the ocean floor after dying.

They were covered by minerals, remains of shells, sediment brought in by the rivers, dust...

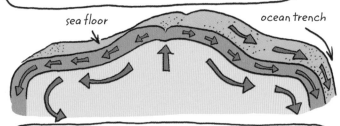

sea floor

ocean trench

Plate tectonics, acting like a conveyor belt, dragged all this toward the depths.

The mineral part compacted to become the BEDROCK. The organic part decomposed under the effect of heat to produce gas, oil (the future petroleum), and a residue resembling unusable coal.

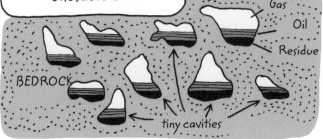

Gas

Oil

Residue

BEDROCK

tiny cavities

Most often, gas and oil emerge from the source rock when it is under pressure—like a squeezed sponge—and migrate to the surface.

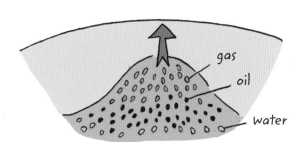

gas

oil

water

Usually, this migration runs its course, and upon reaching the surface:

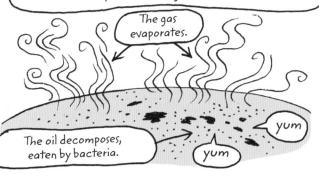

The gas evaporates.

The oil decomposes, eaten by bacteria.

yum

yum

But now and then, the migration is interrupted when it encounters *impermeable rock*...

impermeable rock

reservoir rock — gas

bedrock

The elements are held in a reservoir known as a petroleum trap.

All we have to do is collect it.

When the oil rush began in the United States, the first wells were shallow, and the pressure of the gas made them eruptive.

Yeehah!

Drake used simple water pumps to extract the oil.

Is it like an underground lake?

No. It permeates the reservoir rock.

Picture this: dip a pumice stone in oil...

Then ask your neighbor to bury it 15 feet underground in your garden when you're not looking.

No peeking!

OK, OK!

Once the grass has grown back and covered everything, you go back and try to extract the oil without digging the pumice up, using a straw the size of a sewing needle.

Ptooey!

It's gross!

That's pretty much how we get oil out of the ground.

How about coal?

Coal is formed in much the same way, but from the decomposition of giant ferns in the Carboniferous.

But we'll come back to that later.

coal seams

And all this energy is perfectly renewable...

?

...if you wait, say, 30 to 350 million years.

I know all about your SUVs running on plankton.

Why did we pounce on oil?

We've known about it since Antiquity.

It was mainly collected in places where it came to the surface.

Gross!

The Mesopotamians used its bituminous components to caulk ships.

They knew it was flammable, and were already using it for lamps, but not on a large scale.

In the mid-19th century, the idea of drilling for it, and distilling it on an industrial scale for public and domestic lighting, was born.

Wells had already sprung up in Europe. In the eastern United States, abundant oil at shallow depths caused a rush.

Haha haha

Hahaha

Haha-argh!

Oil saved the whales. Previously, whale oil was used for lighting, even in lighthouses. The need for blubber was so great that whales, especially sperm whales, were almost hunted to extinction. We had to go farther and farther afield to find them.

1861 cartoon from *Vanity Fair* magazine

Petroleum's heavier components were also used to grease steam engines. They replaced vegetable oils.

Oil was used to develop the coal-based industry, before being used as fuel for engines.

SHALE OIL

But one new kind of oil is of particular interest to us:

So-called "shale oil" is misnamed because the rock it comes from is not always shale.

It is also called BEDROCK PETROLEUM.

Because the bedrock is impermeable, oil and gas remain trapped in it.

We can't migrate to the surface.

We're stuck here like suckers.

Sucks

We've known about this oil for a long time.

But we've only really been exploiting it since 2008.

water table

In order to extract a maximum of oil, drilling must turn a corner and penetrate the rock lengthwise.

200-300 m deep

BEDROCK

Three things are injected into the rock: pressurized water to cause fractures, sand to keep the fractures open, and detergent to thin the oil.

This process—known as fracking—requires far more resources than extracting conventional oil.

This ain't no cakewalk.

These wells are mainly found in Texas, New Mexico, and North Dakota.

The wells aren't nearly as productive as normal wells.

A year after startup, production can dwindle by a factor of 5, even 10.

Since the wells put out for such a short period of time, installing a pipeline isn't worth it. The oil is distributed by truck.

Which entails building a network of roads all around.

Here's a view of it from above.

When you find bedrock oil somewhere, there's a good chance you'll find more right next door.

So you drill, you start again, and so on.

The small squares are each the size of a soccer field.

Ah, the pretty features of the wide-open Texan spaces.

Shale oil's energy yield is much lower than that of conventional oil.

Often a lighter oil, it contains a narrower range of exploitable products.

<u>Conventional oil</u>

1 barrel → lets us produce → 100 barrels

<u>Bedrock oil</u>

10 to 20 barrels → lets us produce → 100 barrels

Gas
Naphtha
Gasoline
Kerosene
Diesel
Heating oil
Bitumen

Conventional oil

Bedrock oil

In 2020, frackers stopped investing to cut their losses. And production dropped off...

This is a piece of shit.

Shale oil's price per barrel has hardly ever covered all its costs.

What kinda stupid oil is this, anyway?

The International Energy Agency tells us that in 2008, conventional world oil production passed its peak.

THIIIRSTYYY!!

This leaves us with only shale oil to maintain growing production.

Scrapin' the bottom of the barrel.

Exactly.

There's another kind of bottom-barrel oil...

TAR SANDS.

These are mainly in the Canadian province of Alberta, and Venezuela.

Unlike shale oil, this is oil that has migrated to the surface, where it has accumulated in sand. It has lost its most volatile components to become a kind of bitumen.

Extraction sites resemble open-pit mines. We raze everything that was there before, and stroll merrily on in.

Prospecting for oil is like hunting for Easter eggs in your backyard.

You find the biggest, least well-hidden ones first.

Ha ha ha!

Drake →

PETROLEUM SEEP

EASY PEASY

Then...

Damn it!

Deep-water oil

Shale oil

Tar sands

Shit!

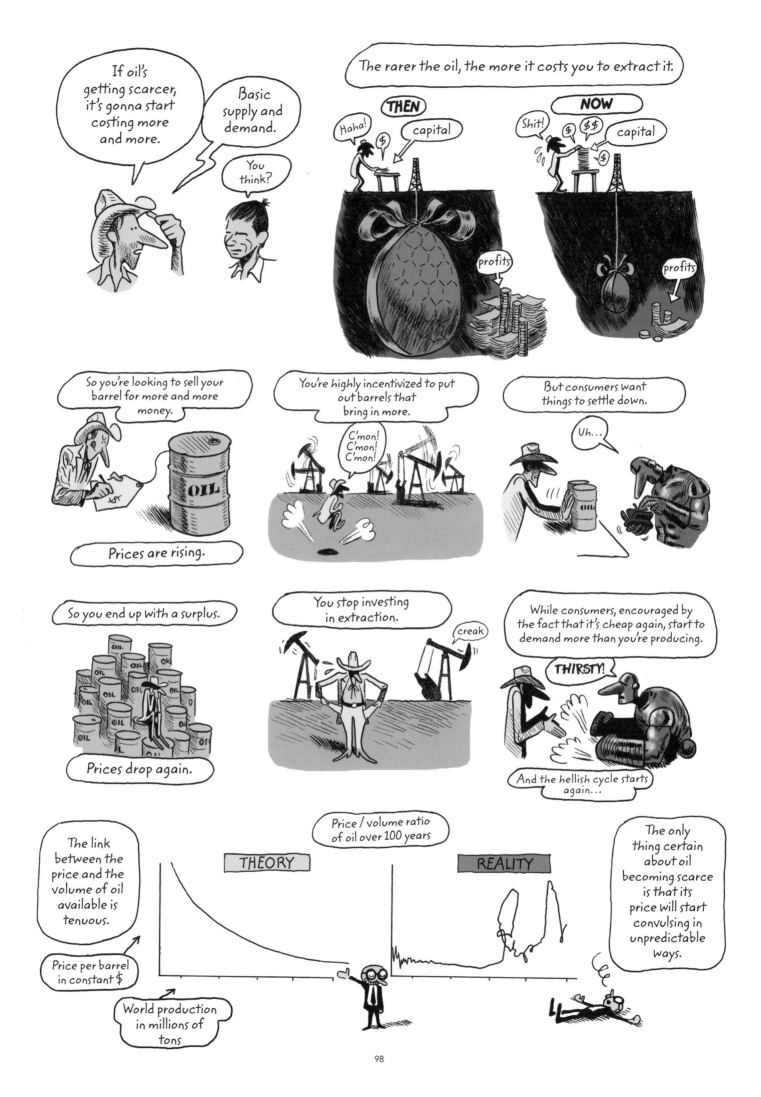

Maybe production is decreasing because it doesn't bring oil companies enough money.

They're less motivated to find new oil.

Yes, at some point, you'll have found all the Easter eggs in the yard.

Search all you want, but you won't find any more.

2004

Big oil invests *$70 billion* to extract *17 billion barrels* per year.

2014

Big oil invests *$300 billion* to extract *14 billion barrels* per year

The hallmark of oil scarcity isn't price, but rather the amount of investment required to extract it.

Big oil is mainly investing to try and limit the decline.

We'll always be trying to extract oil, no matter the cost.

Because he needs to be fed.

HUNGRY!

No?

Right... Energy is what feeds the machines. It's what drives production.

Oil is the medium of exchange among machines.

VRRR

Vroom

The economy is organized around transportation.

VRRR

VRRR

YOGURT FACTORY

YOGURT

MILK

Vroom

YOGURT PLANT

YOGURT

vroom

SUPERMARKET

VR

vroom

vroom

vroom

In France, 80% of people commute to work by car.

Will that figure change after COVID-19?

vroom

vroom

vroom

The economy's dependence on transportation is *absolute.*

Aren't LPG* cars cleaner?

Yes, they pollute a little less...

In theory.

LPG

VROM

* Liquefied petroleum gas

It's not easy using gas for transportation.

1 m³ of oil → 10,000 kWh

1 m³ of gas → 10 kWh

Poser.

Natural gas production is likely to remain marginal.

Natural gas engines are less efficient and consume more. This cancels out the benefit in CO_2 emissions.

LPG

Their tanks are heavy and cumbersome, with safety valves that are complicated to handle.

Gas is hard to transport and store.

You either need a pipe...

Or an LNG carrier.

liquefaction plant

regasification plant

LPG forms in the same places as oil. It was a problem for the oilmen because deposits were often far from the sites of consumption.

Interest in LPG grew after the oil crises.

The oil companies themselves pushed for LPG vehicles to be made. Two percent of the refineries' output consisted of liquefied petroleum gas and they didn't know what to do with it.

What is this crap?

Unload it for me fast, boys.

Quite a few things created for completely unrelated reasons are later presented to us as environmental improvements.

For example, Iran has the world's second largest reserves of natural gas, but imports it instead to supply its large northern cities.

Installing enough gas pipelines crossing the country would be too costly.

Natural gas is essentially a regional source of energy. It takes a long-term agreement, with regulations between producer and consumer countries, to secure it.

Natural gas is used for stationary appliances.

 → Heating ~30%

 → Industrial ovens ~30%

 → Electricity production ~40%

But it's still a fossil fuel. It contributes to CO_2 emissions.

You're gross!

Oh yeah?!

No kidding.

11% of CO_2 emissions

20% of CO_2 emissions

At any rate, its reserves follow the same path as that of oil.

Peak natural gas production will occur 10-20 years after that of oil's.

ZIP

ZILCH

NADA

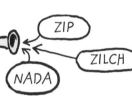

What about coal?

Historically, it is the oldest fossil energy.

It first replaced wood, in forges, heaters, and steam engines.

But today, 2/3 of the world's coal is used to produce electricity.

And 35% of the world's electricity is made with coal.

There's a Chinese joke that says by the time a coal-hauling train gets to where it's going, everything it's hauling will already be gone.

empty   empty   Sorry.

It's very heavy for the amount of energy it provides.

A coal-fired car wouldn't be powerful enough to carry its own tank.

It worked with boats...

...because they glide on water.

And trains...

...because rails don't generate much friction.

Since it's hard to transport, this is the only model for international trade.

Mines

Near the shore

Coastal power plant

But it's not very common.

Since coal use is primarily electrical, power plants are close to the mines.

Will we reach peak coal too?

Scarcity isn't the most worrisome thing about coal.

The real worry here is its potential, as the most carbon-intensive energy, to destroy the climate.

We'll be burnt to a cinder before we have to worry about running out of coal.

There's a lot of coal in the world, but over 3/4 of it is located in only 5 countries.

USA

CHINA

RUSSIA

AUSTRALIA

INDIA

We know how to make synthetic oil from coal. But it's a lower-quality fuel. And the transformation process consumes half the coal.

Hitler powered his planes with coal oil during the Battle of Britain.

Haha!

The Spitfires flew with good oil supplied by the Americans.

It gave them a huge advantage over the nevertheless efficient Messerschmitt.

Scheiße!

Like oil, the deeper the coal is buried, the better its quality. It's been "cooked" for longer in the depths.

Surface coal is mediocre coal.

This is the case with lignite, exploited today in Germany.

Lignite is used extensively to produce electricity.

To access it, the Germans had to remove everything on the surface: houses, forests, vegetation.

60% of the world's electricity production comes from fossil fuels.

Coal — 34%
Natural gas — 23%
Oil — 3%

40% of global emissions (33% just from coal)

I'm the grossest of 'em all!

In recent years, fossil fuel use has increased the most, in colossal proportions.

Loser!

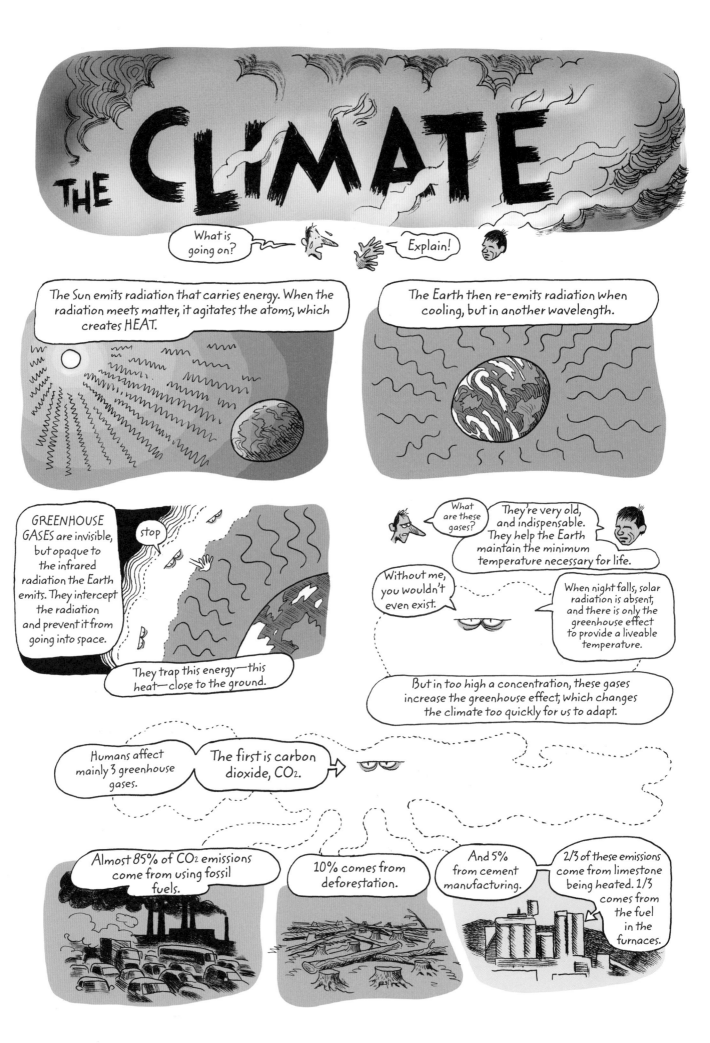

THE CLIMATE

What is going on?

Explain!

The Sun emits radiation that carries energy. When the radiation meets matter, it agitates the atoms, which creates HEAT.

The Earth then re-emits radiation when cooling, but in another wavelength.

GREENHOUSE GASES are invisible, but opaque to the infrared radiation the Earth emits. They intercept the radiation and prevent it from going into space.

stop

They trap this energy—this heat—close to the ground.

What are these gases?

They're very old, and indispensable. They help the Earth maintain the minimum temperature necessary for life.

Without me, you wouldn't even exist.

When night falls, solar radiation is absent, and there is only the greenhouse effect to provide a liveable temperature.

But in too high a concentration, these gases increase the greenhouse effect, which changes the climate too quickly for us to adapt.

Humans affect mainly 3 greenhouse gases.

The first is carbon dioxide, CO_2.

Almost 85% of CO_2 emissions come from using fossil fuels.

10% comes from deforestation.

And 5% from cement manufacturing.

2/3 of these emissions come from limestone being heated. 1/3 comes from the fuel in the furnaces.

Water vapor is another greenhouse gas, almost entirely emitted naturally.

Since oceans cover 2/3 of the planet, they form a huge evaporation machine. In comparison, direct human emissions of water vapor are negligible.

But we do influence this indirectly. The higher the surface temperature, the more evaporation occurs.

How long does it stay in the atmosphere?

Just a few days, but it's always being renewed.

The higher temperatures rise, the more water vapor the atmosphere can contain.

The greenhouse effect will just get worse. It'll be even hotter.

The hotter it gets, the hotter it gets.

Imagine a planet with an excess of CO_2 in its atmosphere that raises the average ground temperature by 1.5°C... The presence of water vapor causes an amplification effect that raises that warming from 1.5 to 4°C.

But you can't make the atmosphere absorb an infinite amount of water vapor, because it condenses. Then it rains.

Rain is life.

Yes, but it doesn't necessarily rain where people are.

The monsoons will be more intense.

But ... so will the dry seasons.

Rainfall will have a harder time penetrating the earth. And deforestation favors runoff rather than absorption.

Thirsty!

The hotter it gets, the more water evaporates.

Even with constant precipitation, the soil dries out.

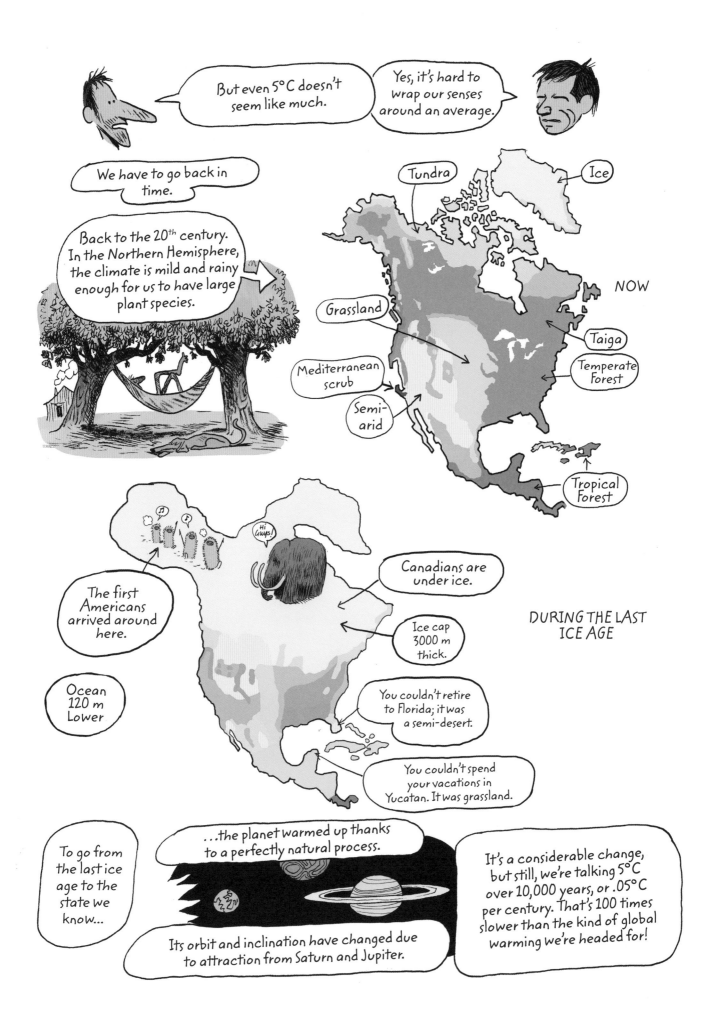

This is the face of a world where the average temperature has risen by 4°C compared to today.

Problem No. 1: the Equator, where relative humidity has reached saturation, affecting over 1/3 of the world's population. When the air's hotter than your skin, you can't regulate your body temperature by sweating, leading to death.

Before their normal lifespan is up, people born today could find themselves in a place where it would be impossible to survive outdoors.

Number of days in the year when you can't survive outdoors

0   50   100   150   200   250   300   350

Now, as for soil moisture...

France is one of the areas that would dry up the most, along with the whole Mediterranean basin.

As the soil dries out, agricultural yields decline.

The population's rising, so the demand for food rises.

Evolution of soil moisture in %

-10   -7.5   -5   -2.5   0   2.5   5   7.5   10

When people have nothing to eat, they move.

There will be major migratory movements.

Nature has another self-regulating protocol prepared: famine.

In this case, the population gets reduced.

Germs love it when you heat their Petri dish. We're already seeing diseases from the hot zones moving up toward the poles.

The CO_2-laden oceans will grow more acidic, which leads to reduced calcification in the shells and exoskeletons of some plankton. Coral reefs, which are home to 25% of marine species, will also suffer. This puts added pressure on marine life. And all this is without mentioning intensive fishing.

Greenland has begun to melt. This will go on no matter what we do, because of inertia in the system.

Sea levels will rise. Many coastal cities will be partially submerged.

Sure, but that's a few generations away. It'll happen very slowly. We'll gradually adapt to it, right?

Water levels have already started rising. Extreme events such as hurricanes and storms will cause damage that will allow the sea to breach such defenses as dikes and dunes. By 2100, these kinds of disasters could become so common as to multiply by a hundredfold along coasts worldwide.

On top of that, the influx of seawater will salinize coastal aquifers.

Permafrost refers to frozen land in places such as Alaska, Siberia, and Canada. It covers 20% of the Earth's surface.

It's begun thawing, releasing CO_2 and methane in quantities still poorly assessed...

...further accelerating global warming.

It could also contain dormant viruses.

The thaw may release unexpected phenomena.

It may also destabilize infrastructure built on top of it, often mining and oil operations. In June 2020, a fuel storage tank at a Norilsk Nickel plant failed, spilling more than 20,000 tons of diesel oil into the surrounding environment.

It was the biggest environmental disaster ever to hit the Arctic.

So which of these will happen first?

And how soon?

There's no way to tell.

We're venturing into uncharted waters...

The picture is very complex.

We can't wait for science to provide minutely detailed descriptions of every danger before getting our asses in gear.

The amount of arable land per capita worldwide has decreased from 4 acres in 1960 to 1.5 today.

It wasn't an issue, because we had tractors, fertilizer, etc...

No problemo.

What happens when, in a world with limited energy, such advantages are no longer so freely available, and the climate becomes even less favorable?

The IPCC report "Climate Change and Land" suggests that at around 3°C of global warming, food insecurity becomes widespread on the planet.

Before 2040, many trees in the forests of temperate countries will die from drought, disease, fire, and insect pests whose populations have soared thanks to global warming.

The excess greenhouse effect keeps heat trapped in the lower atmosphere, preventing the Earth's radiation from rising to the stratosphere to warm it.

50 km
STRATOSPHERE
12 km
TROPOSPHERE
0 km
EARTH

The temperature differential between ground and stratosphere increases, setting in motion even more extreme phenomena.

This affects cyclones, hurricanes, and probably thunderstorms, which may grow more violent.

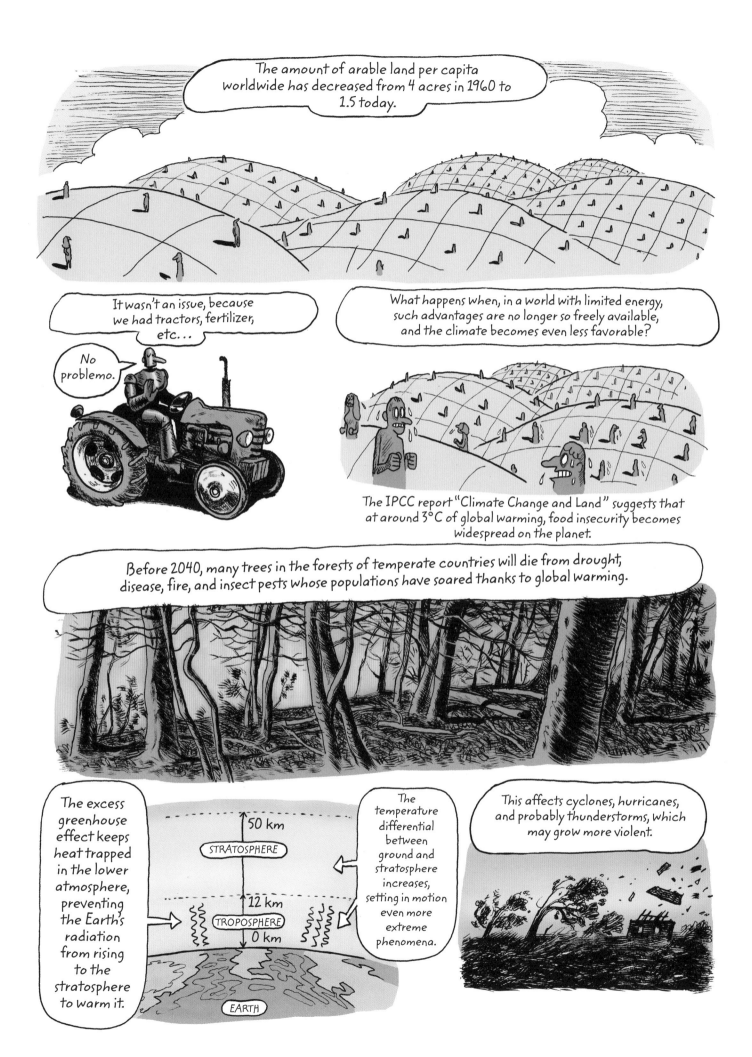

Just a few degrees of warming over 20,000 years changed the face of the Earth. What will a few degrees in one century do on a planet that will increasingly lack the means—that is to say, Armor Man's poison of choice—to face unexpected disturbances?

This is why a hurricane kills 1,500 people in the United States and 140,000 in Bangladesh.

USA

BANGLADESH

My first book was an account of life in Bangladesh right after the April 1991 cyclone.

I know just what you're talking about.

Energy abundance enables us to intervene, with law enforcement, rescue services, evacuations, food provision, and swift reconstruction of people's homes.

This is also what machines are for: to deal with unexpected events.

In a world where resources are becoming progressively limited, the risk is a return to barbarism.

I wasn't a big *Mad Max* fan when I was a kid.

?

It can destroy peace, democracy, and people's ability to feed themselves abundantly and survive.

In reality, massive social upheaval is already underway.

Take, for example, the "Arab Spring" in 2010. It was born of 3 factors...

The drought in the Mediterranean basin, which has since only worsened, preventing local agriculture from feeding a growing population...

The 2008 subprime crisis, which caused tourism to plummet. And export revenues in Tunisia and Egypt crashed.

The price of food imports increased as a result of the drought in Russia—which accounts for 20% of the world's grain market—and the rising price of oil.

This strong economic stress led to the food riots.

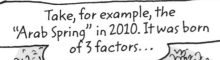

Increasingly severe disruptions like these will become more common. In places like the US, there will be drought after drought.

Satellite photos of Lake Powell

The level of Arizona's Lake Powell will drop spectacularly.

August 2017

August 2020

Forests are already suffering a great deal. Trees are getting weaker in a troubling way.

Drier forests provide conditions conducive to huge fires, like in California and Australia.

The systemic destabilizations of the next 20 years have already been set in motion, thanks to our past emissions. Atmospheric CO_2 is stubbornly persistent.

Been bulking up.

We'll need Armor Man's help.

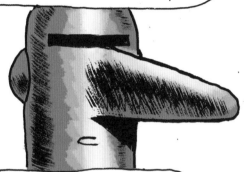

With him on board, we can...

Irrigate with ease, even where it doesn't rain.

Secure our water stores by building reservoirs.

Transport food from where it is grown to where we eat it.

Introduce tree species better adapted to the warming climate (birch and beech cannot survive in the Mediterranean).

Adapt buildings, move populations...

Put up defences to protect seaside dwellings...

But we run into a twofold problem: pollution and dwindling energy supplies.

Too much trash

Empty cupboards

At the end of 2022, our atmospheric emissions totaled 2,450 billion tons of CO_2. This means we've already signed up for 1.3°C of global warming.

Just how intense this warming will be depends on the cumulative amount of greenhouse gases we put into the atmosphere by 2100.

If you don't want more than 2°C of warming, I'm not allowed to weigh more than 3,000 billion tons.

So I can't put on more than 550 billion tons.

But hey, it's up to you.

I may be invisible, but I swing my weight around.

550 billion is roughly one quarter of what we've already put out.

And that's enabled our purchasing power, pensions, and higher education to exist.

Greenhouse gas emissions must be reduced by at least 2/3 by 2050. That is to say, a decrease of 5% per year.

In other words, Armor Man's hooch and fossil fritters have to drop by 4% or more yearly.

Huh?!

Aw, shit!

In practical terms, this means an extra COVID-19 pandemic every year.

Ha ha ha!

Do you think any nation in the world has really grasped what this means?

Any Congressmen?

We've only just touched on what it means to reduce emissions at the right speed.

Remember, we have to reduce emissions by 2/3 by 2050.

The question is how.

By reducing the population by 2/3?

Famine and disease will do it. War will have a harder time... unless it facilitates famine and disease. The Spanish flu in 1918 killed more people faster than World War II. The great plague of the 14th century cut the population in half. This is pretty heavy stuff...

Otherwise, there's also birth control.

Delicate subject...

Wouldn't touch it...

Going by demographic projections—which are only projections—we can expect the population to increase by a factor of 1.2 by 2050. Unless there is a lethal pandemic...

Or a good old meteorite.

The remaining terms must now be divided not by 3 but by 3.6... Let's start with per capita GDP. Who will be OK with this? Every country in the world is hoping for a growth of at least 2% per year.

growth growth growth growth gro growth growth uu growth growth growth growth growth growth growth

Non-carbon energies

Wind and solar energy are the symbols of "good" energy. They're recent and represent a tiny share in world use: 1.6% for solar, 2.8% for wind.

For now, if you recall, non-carbon energies like wind, solar, hydropower, and nuclear do not replace any other kind of energy.

We use them on top of "bad" energies...

Whose use has only gone up, barring bumps in the road.

good

bad

bad

bad

bad

COAL OIL GAS

It's as if Bluebeard were knocking off more and more women...

...but giving to charity at the same time.

For the poor...

Thank you, M'lord.

Much progress has been made in exploiting renewable energies. A wind turbine is more advanced than a windmill and the domestic use of solar energy has only existed since the early 1970s. But it requires lots of resources and space to function.

Can I plug in my cell phone?

Were wind to provide all the energy in the US, we'd have to plant a wind turbine every mile and a half across the whole country, regardless of how windy or unsuitable the terrain might be.

You'd be completely surrounded by wind turbines as soon as you left any city.

There wouldn't be a spot without one.

There are 2 types of electrical production.

Dispatchable generation, supplying on demand.

for your cold beer

or your knee surgery

And non-dispatchable generation, existing only when external conditions are met.

no wind

warm beer

So... come back tomorrow for your knee? High-pressure system today.

Were the US to depend entirely on renewables for its electricity...

...you'd have to supplement the wind.

Dispatchable production includes hydropower. Turn on the tap in the reservoir and run the turbine! Or...imagine building a big seawater reserve along the coast...

For a backup supply, say 2 weeks' worth of power generation, the dam would look like this:

100 m

100 m

The dam would run the length of the coast and be 150 m high.

NEW YORK

We can't even see the Statue of Liberty...

Another example, Venezuela's Guri Dam, has a surface area of 1,641 sq. mi., two thirds of the size of Los Angeles.

Which is the sixth biggest in the world.

Guri has the power of 10 nuclear reactors...

...but takes up 2-3 thousand times more space.

Still, hydropower isn't as dangerous as nuclear, right?

Twenty years ago, when I first began to delve into these issues, climate change was the first thing to catch my attention.

We're screwed!

Then I started looking at energy sources that did not emit CO_2.

What the heck is this thing...?

It took me years to wrap my head around it and really understand it.

What in the blazes?

I feel like you're about to sell me on nuclear plants.

They're not the whole answer.

What's fundamentally at stake in this discussion is rearranging our priorities.

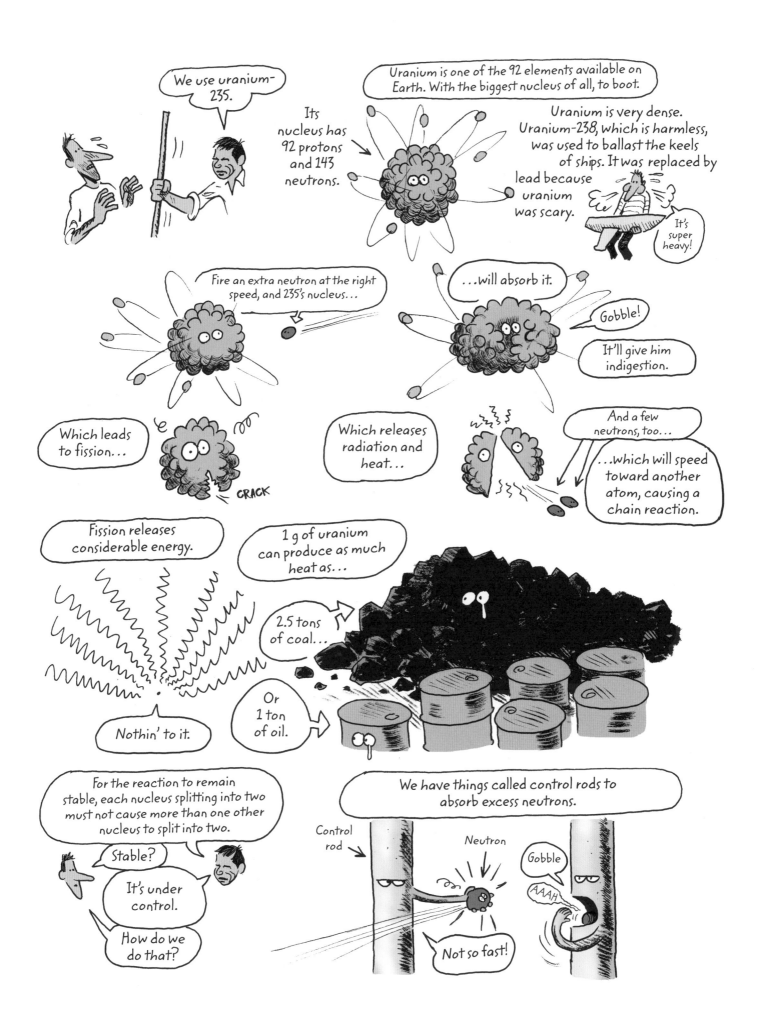

Almost every Western nuclear reactor requires uranium-235 at just over 3% to maintain efficient fission. Naturally occurring uranium contains only 0.8%. As a result, we must enrich it.

In machines like these.

At 3%, there's no risk of explosion. It takes concentrations of over 99% to make a bomb.

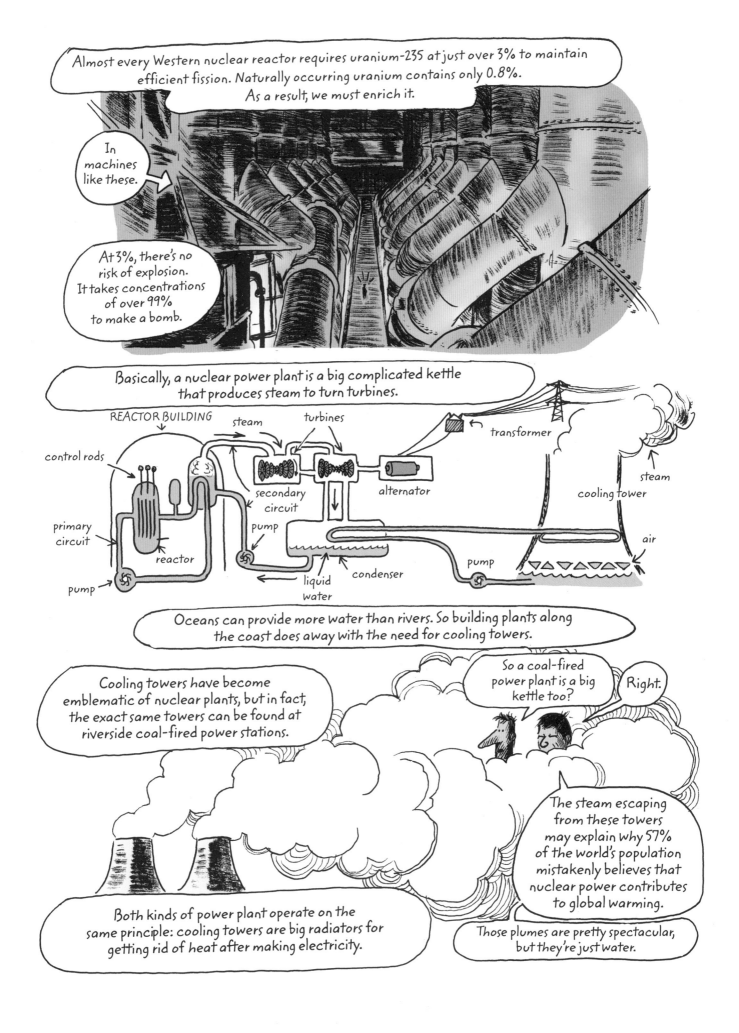

Basically, a nuclear power plant is a big complicated kettle that produces steam to turn turbines.

REACTOR BUILDING

control rods

primary circuit

reactor

pump

steam

turbines

secondary circuit

pump

liquid water

condenser

alternator

transformer

pump

cooling tower

steam

air

Oceans can provide more water than rivers. So building plants along the coast does away with the need for cooling towers.

Cooling towers have become emblematic of nuclear plants, but in fact, the exact same towers can be found at riverside coal-fired power stations.

So a coal-fired power plant is a big kettle too?

Right.

The steam escaping from these towers may explain why 57% of the world's population mistakenly believes that nuclear power contributes to global warming.

Both kinds of power plant operate on the same principle: cooling towers are big radiators for getting rid of heat after making electricity.

Those plumes are pretty spectacular, but they're just water.

130

Wind and solar have a nice image…

…because they draw energy in what seems like the most natural way.

A 1 billion-watt reactor (1 gigawatt)

3 hectares

Highly concentrated energy; a very small amount of matter produces a large amount of energy.

A 1 GW solar power plant

1,000 hectares

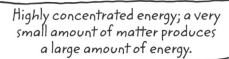

Diffuse energy; it requires so much space that it starts encroaching on forests, crops, and protected areas.

Because of their very diffuse nature, solar and wind power require 10 to 100 times more metal per kWh…

…and 10 to 100 times more cement.

12 to 15 m

3 to 4 m

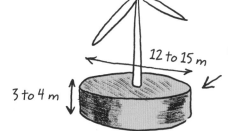

Wind turbines are anchored in concrete foundations flush with the ground. These sometimes remain once the turbine is dismantled.

Nuclear power requires mines for extracting uranium, energy to enrich it, and concrete for the plant itself. But nuclear energy is so concentrated that in the end, we emit very little CO_2 per kWh produced.

Vroom

For power plants, there is an important concept called THE LOAD FACTOR. For example, a gas- or coal-fired power plant generally produces as much power per year as if it had been running continuously at half its maximum capacity. Its load factor is then said to be 50%.

NUCLEAR POWER PLANT

Dispatchable

Load factor: 60-90%

6 g of CO_2 per kWh

Lifespan: 60 years

COAL-FIRED POWER PLANT

Dispatchable

Load factor: 20-90%

800-1,000 g of CO_2 per kWh

Lifespan: 40-60 years

GAS POWER PLANT

Dispatchable

Load factor: 20-80%

400 g of CO_2 per kWh

Lifespan: 40 years

HYDROPOWER

Dispatchable

Load factor: 25-50%, country-dependent

6 g of CO_2 per kWh

Lifespan: 200 years

WIND POWER

Non-Dispatchable

Load factor: 20-30% on land, 40% at sea

10 g of CO_2 per kWh

Lifespan: 20-30 years

SOLAR

Non-dispatchable

Load factor: approx. 15% in Maine, 25% in Southern California.

20-50 g of CO_2 per kWh

Lifespan: 30 years

Is there a loss when storing electricity?

 From 20 to 40%.

Which means a corresponding increase in resources and production.

Batteries require more metallurgy and chemistry.

But we have to make them to store electricity.

 50g of CO_2 per kWh stored and returned

 Fine, nuclear's more efficient. But...

When I was a kid, my grandparents lived right by a nuclear plant on the bank of a river.

I had recurring nightmares about the area being evacuated because of a nuclear accident. For some obscure reason, I'd have to go back there all alone to recover something vital I'd left behind...

I ran and ran...

Couldn't feel a thing...

Couldn't see a thing, but I was scared of contamination.

HA HA HA! Now I see why you said this book was a kind of therapy for you.

Um... Jean-Marc, what is radioactivity? Y'know, when those invisible rays pass through you...

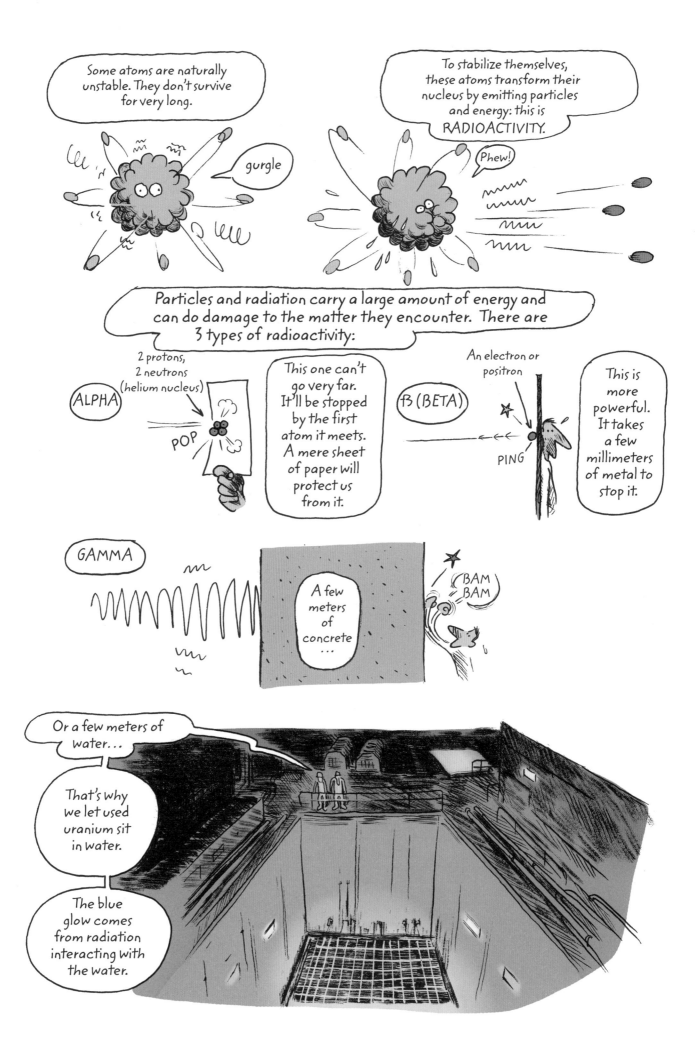

Some atoms are naturally unstable. They don't survive for very long.

gurgle

To stabilize themselves, these atoms transform their nucleus by emitting particles and energy: this is RADIOACTIVITY.

Phew!

Particles and radiation carry a large amount of energy and can do damage to the matter they encounter. There are 3 types of radioactivity:

2 protons, 2 neutrons (helium nucleus)

ALPHA

POP

This one can't go very far. It'll be stopped by the first atom it meets. A mere sheet of paper will protect us from it.

An electron or positron

β (BETA)

PING

This is more powerful. It takes a few millimeters of metal to stop it.

GAMMA

A few meters of concrete ...

BAM BAM

Or a few meters of water...

That's why we let used uranium sit in water.

The blue glow comes from radiation interacting with the water.

134

The potential damage from radioactivity is measured in sieverts.

In the US, natural radioactivity is a few thousandths of a sievert.

NATURAL RADIATION

3 mSV (milli-sieverts) per year

AH!

Rest assured, at this level, it's totally harmless.

The higher up you go, the less protection you have from cosmic radiation.

An airline crew takes in between 5 and 20 mSV per year.

We're still at a level that doesn't matter.

In a space station, you're no longer protected by the atmosphere. Astronauts are certainly among the most irradiated people you can find.

I don't care!

I want more!

180 mSV for 6 months in space.

Many rocks are naturally radioactive. For example, people living on granitic soil get a bit more radioactive exposure.

But Yosemite's or New Hampshire's granitic soils have nothing on India's thorium-containing monazite sands. People in Kerala get from 50 to 100 mSV per year.

Yet, life expectancy there is higher than in the rest of the country.

A CT scan will get you between 10 and 20 mSV.

Starting at 5 to 10 SV, chances are you'll soon die.

ARG

But under 200 mSV annually, there's no observable effect, even in the long term.

I'm not glowing!

Sometimes a high-dose of radioactivity can actually heal us. Radiation therapy involves sending a dose of a few dozen to a few hundred sieverts to destroy a tumor.

In the vicinity of a power plant, ambient radioactivity increases by 0.02 mSV.

But what if it blows up?

What happened in Chernobyl?

In Chernobyl, they built an inherently dangerous reactor.

It's very different from the present-day reactors you'll find in France and in most countries around the world.

Remember, neutrons must be slowed down so they can be captured by uranium atoms and cause fission.

Otherwise, it's like trying to eat a peanut with a slingshot.

Uranium atom

Neutron peanut

Typical water reactor

Water has 2 roles.

It slows down or "moderates" the neutrons…

…and it evacuates heat.

This design has what is called "passive safety." If you lose the cooling water (because of a leak, for example), the neutrons aren't slowed anymore, and fission stops.

Chernobyl-type reactor

Here, the 2 functions were separated.

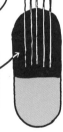

Graphite was used as a moderator.

Lose the water cooling the reactor, and the moderator remains, but the reaction gets out of control and overheats. You no longer have passive safety.

To top it all off, there was a design flaw in the control rods.

Это что за херня*?

* What the hell is this?

Sounds like a reactor from hell!

Those reactors usually date back to the early days of civil nuclear power. In the West, they have been shut down or, as in the UK, they soon will be.

Why were they ever made?

136

Those kinds of reactors were built because they could also produce weapons-grade plutonium.

To obtain this "high quality" plutonium, you have to be able to load and unload the fuel continuously, which entails safeguards being removed.

The great majority of power-generating reactors have no military function. Every 12 to 18 months, they're shut down for 1 or 2 months so the fuel can be replaced.

At Chernobyl, operators were specifically asked to disconnect the safety systems to test the behavior of the reactor outside its normal zone.

You mean they went looking for trouble?

The experiment went wrong. The reaction got out of hand.

Graphite

Fuel

The metal of the tubes containing the uranium pellets (zirconium) reacted with the superheated steam and created large quantities of hydrogen that accumulated in the reactor vessel.

The hydrogen and oxygen in the air formed an explosive mixture.

БУМ!

After the explosion, the graphite and the molten core were exposed to the open air.

The graphite ignited upon contact with the air. The fire vaporized part of the reactor core a few kilometers up in the air.

There are at least 2 reasons why no such accident could happen again:

①— There is no graphite in the core of most reactors around the world.

②— In France, a second security measure has been developed: a "hydrogen recombiner."

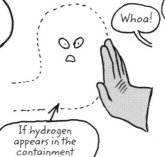

Whoa!

It gets recombined with oxygen...

To make water.

If hydrogen appears in the containment structure...

hydrogen oxygen

How many people died?

Do you know UNSCEAR?

Un-what?

Or the IPCC?

?

Intergovernmental Panel on Climate Change.

A UN body created in 1988.

Its mandate is to synthesize everything published in scientific literature on the impact of human activity on the climate.

Bravo!

Climate research is so prolific that thousands of pages are being published in peer-reviewed journals.

Naturally, no one has time to read all of them.

So the IPCC's job is to compile it.

In a 5,000-page report...

HNGH...

...a technical summary of 300 pages...

...and a 20-page brief for decision makers.

UNSCEAR (United Nations Scientific Committee on the Effects of Atomic Radiation) does the same thing for radioactivity.

Are there as many pages?

Same order of magnitude.

Doctors and biologists have been studying the subject for over 100 years.

UNSCEAR is 30 years older. We've known for a long time that radioactivity can do damage.

Marie Curie died of it.

Of course, UNSCEAR has produced reports on Chernobyl and Fukushima.

For Chernobyl, the conclusions are as follows: it caused about thirty deaths over a short period. Basically, the first people who fought the fire...

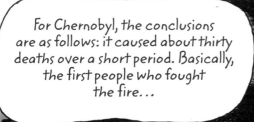

6,000 people who were children at the time of the accident developed thyroid cancer.

Luckily, this is a form of cancer that can be treated effectively.

As for the rest: surprising as it may seem, there are no health consequences that are outside the norm.

Are you sure we got full info in the Soviet era?

There are a few gray areas...

But we can evaluate what escaped at the time of the accident with measurements made well after the fact.

WHAT?!

That doesn't seem like much!

It surprised me too.

Took me a while to get my head around it.

CRRR CRRR

Is UNSCEAR above suspicion?

Money from oil and gas, the world's richest industry, could not buy the few thousand scientists who write up the IPCC reports.

$ $ $ $
$ $ $ $
$ $ $
?

Can you seriously imagine that the nuclear industry, with 100 times less money, could corrupt 10 to 100 times more scientists, doctors, and biologists?

Not to mention that many of them come from countries without a nuclear industry, or even some that are against having one.

$
?

You mean Chernobyl wasn't all that bad?

NO! It was a **CATASTROPHE!**

Stress from the accident and the evacuation of the population had dramatic consequences. This is also in the UNSCEAR report.

In fact, panic and fear of radioactivity did more damage than the radioactivity itself.

The collapse of the Soviet bloc came soon after the accident. The breakdown of the health-care system and the increase in risky behaviors, such as smoking and alcohol, were proven factors in the decline of life expectancy.

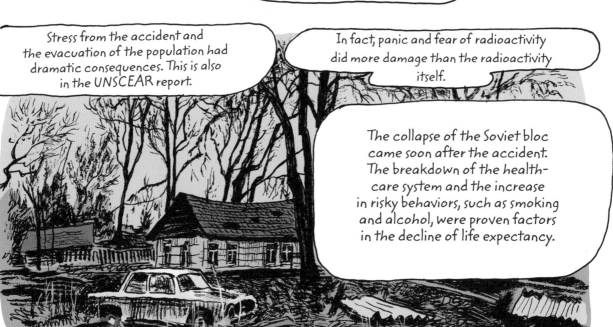

Paradoxically, Chernobyl has now become a nature reserve for large animals that had almost disappeared.

For the wildlife, there's no contest between the benefits from evacuating the people and the inconveniences linked to radiation.

What happened there?

Their reactor was designed differently from ours in France, using boiling water instead of pressurized water. This means that there's only one water circuit instead of two.

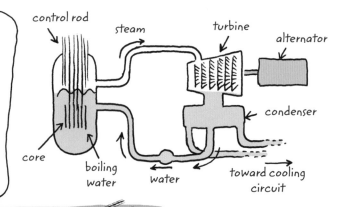

control rod

steam

turbine

alternator

condenser

core

boiling water

water

toward cooling circuit

First, there was a violent earthquake.

The reactor went into "safe mode." The control rods fell inside and fission stopped instantly. But the heat from the core's internal radioactivity didn't.

An hour after shutdown, the core was still heating at 1% of its maximum power.

It doesn't sound like much, but it's the equivalent of 15,000 large radiators in a very small volume.

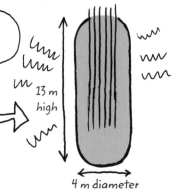

13 m high

4 m diameter

Water circulation had to be maintained to cool it down.

But the earthquake had damaged the entire electrical system around the plant.

Generators took over to power the pumps that kept the water flowing.

Then a tsunami hit, 30 minutes after the earthquake.

The diesel generators were designed to withstand up to 6 m waves, but waves 10 m high had already been known to hit the area.

The tsunami had 14-m waves.

The emergency diesels were flooded.

The cooling system stopped cooling, and the water in it gradually vaporized. Part of the core was no longer immersed and started getting very hot. That's when the zirconium cladding began to crack and let fission by-products escape...

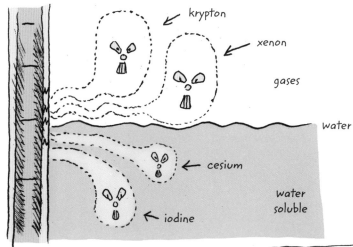

krypton

xenon

gases

water

cesium

water soluble

iodine

Zirconium reacts with water vapor, producing *hydrogen*...

If I meet oxygen, I explode!

The pressure in the reactor vessel was rising. It needed depressurizing to prevent rupture...

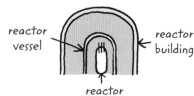

reactor vessel

reactor building

reactor

After depressurization, hydrogen escaped into the reactor building ...

air

In the reactor building, there was air...

In the air, there was oxygen...

The building's roof has blown clean off!

Radioactive waste ran hog wild in the surrounding environment.

ドトーン

This chain of events could never happen in France.

Remember, our nuclear plants have hydrogen recombiners.

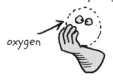

oxygen

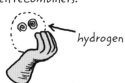

hydrogen

And the containment buildings have sand filters to prevent radioactive elements from escaping.

STOP

After Fukushima, France created a nuclear rapid action force (FARN).

In France, our cheeses stink...

Not our power stations.

143

Chernobyl, just like Fukushima, prompted nuclear operators to improve their safety systems.

You mustn't think that everyone in the civil nuclear industry is some kind of Sith Lord, trying to get the biggest bullshit they can off the ground.

Er...

We've set it all so it'll blow up right in their faces, Lord Vader!

HHH

Good.

You're saying Chernobyl and Fukushima only had local repercussions?

More important than local consequences the global psychological impact is!

For example, the way the Germans reacted after Fukushima will prove thousands of times deadlier than all our nuclear accidents combined.

NEIN!

Immediate impact: FEAR

water vapor nix

Immediate impact: fine particle pollution, deforestation, biodiversity loss (due to lignite coal mining)

Long-term impact: global warming, ocean acidification, lower crop yields, death of coral reefs, etc.

Wir haben auch Windkraftanlagen.*

Ja!

Had the Germans kept their nuclear power plants after Fukushima instead of switching to lignite and coal, they'd have avoided emitting 800 million tons of CO_2 by late 2021: that is to say, a whole year's worth of emissions for their country.

* We also have wind turbines.

Nuclear power is a bit like air travel. Accidents are attention-grabbing and create a sense of dread.

There were over 4 billion civil aviation passengers in 2017 and no deaths on commercial airliners. There were 283 deaths in 2019.

There are 3,700 car deaths per day worldwide. That's 7 crowded Boeing 747 crashes. This amounts to 1.35 million deaths per year.

We can respond to fear of nuclear power in two ways:

① So long, nuclear plants, so long, fear of nuclear plants.

Reminds me of my tree-hugging cousins from when I was a kid in the '70s. They were super nice, drove an old Volkswagen Kombi...

② Far longer, far more complicated, and often far more arduous: tell people what the real risks are compared to the benefits.

ATOMKRAFT? NEIN DANKE

my cousin is German

ha ha

What's this sticker over here mean?

Nuclear? No thanks!

Emits almost no CO_2

Produces little waste since it uses very little material compared to the energy it supplies

Makes you less dependent on foreign countries than fossil fuels do

Is dispatchable

METRO
NO METRO TODAY NOT ENOUGH WIND

And my surgery?

Just waiting for a breeze.

No thanks.

OIL

GAZ

Atomkraft, nein danke.

Global warming, biodiversity loss, ocean acidification, mass migration, disease, devastated forests, massive fires, submerged coastal areas, wars...

Nein danke.

The water table is 20 m down.

...unless a volcano appears right on the spot.

Due to gravity, any pollution comes from above, not below.

Nitrates, traces of phytosanitary products, filth from industrial activity, etc.— these can be found there.

400 m

1 m of dirt stops any radioactivity cold. There is no chance that even the slightest ounce of artificial radioactivity can make its way up...

radioactive waste — concrete

Chances of this seem, well... low.

How much uranium is left?

Enough to run the current plants for a few hundred years...

I know that smile. You're about to completely freak me out.

But not enough to sustainably replace all coal-fired power stations.

I knew it! We're screwed!

No, the uranium we have can be used far more efficiently.

Breeder reactors or not, nuclear power is a competitor to coal. Every year, coal kills the equivalent of half the population of Boston worldwide, just among miners and former miners.

I'm not even talking about particulate matter...

When winter brings a high pressure system to France, with a northeasterly wind, a broad swath of the country receives particles from German and Polish coal-fired power stations.

KOF

All modern technologies cause deaths. Nuclear power is among those that cause the fewest. Far fewer than backyard swimming pools.

It's statistically safer to take your kids on a tour of a nuclear power plant than to leave them alone by the pool.

Why do some authorities want to reduce nuclear power so badly, then?

The authorities pander to an inordinate fear of nuclear power rooted in a lack of understanding.

They choose demagogy over pedagogy.

It's as if the majority of the population were convinced that burning witches was advantageous to the common good. The state knows vaguely that this isn't the case, but still burns one every now and then anyway.

Burn!

Burn!

Burn!

Burn, fission lovers!

Burn!

Criminal cynicism!

Rather, comfortable ignorance.

Basically, information about the advantages and disadvantages of nuclear power is readily available, but it's more comfortable to ignore it.

When you've made a reputation by fighting nuclear power in the name of the environment, it's hard to dig deeper and admit you were wrong.

You risk alienating your voter base.

I agree with Janco on everything.

Except for nuclear power.

Deep down, you think he's not entirely wrong about nuclear power.

Are you cuckoo?!

The anti-nukers are my native habitat. If I cut myself off from my habitat, I'll *die!*

No thanks!

No!

Nuclear? No thanks!

Atomkraft, nein danke!

No!

No!

No thanks!

Nuclear no thanks!

You're right.

Monopolies are bad.

Is a monopoly always bad?

Competition is made to create uncertainty. Uncertainty stimulates creativity and competition. But it encourages short-termism.

CHUG ♪

HOSPITAL

This is major infrastructure that requires enormous resources to be implemented.

We speak of a "natural monopoly" because it doesn't make sense to have multiple copies of them in the same niche.

Hmm... which water is cheapest today?

Somewhere in Great Britain...

If you go for it anyway, experience has shown that such systems don't work as well and cost more.

Ahem... Sorry, sir... Do you know when the train is coming?

If it's coming...

155

What do we do now?

One of two things.

Either we go back to a society dependent on the elements. You are treated or fed when there is wind, sun, or rain...

Or else we try to maintain dispatchable renewable energy.

We could replace nuclear power with wind and solar power, if we make them dispatchable.

batteries

Can we do this peacefully with 8 billion people living on the planet?

Provided that devices are supplemented with storage.

Today, the combined electrical power of all the means of production is over 7,000 GW.

The available storage capacity is 160 GW. 99% of it comes from reversible dams.

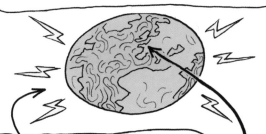

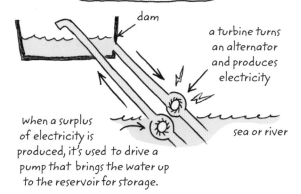

dam

a turbine turns an alternator and produces electricity

when a surplus of electricity is produced, it's used to drive a pump that brings the water up to the reservoir for storage.

sea or river

The estimated earthly reserves of lithium (the highest-performing battery metal) would allow us to store one week of global electrical production in batteries (with their capacity declining over time).

If we used wind and solar energy alone to produce electricity in France, we'd need 2.5 tons of batteries per household (2.2 people for an average of 60 m^2) costing 50,000€ and with a lifespan of 10 years.

This storage can hold only 2% of the world's production power, roughly 140 GW.

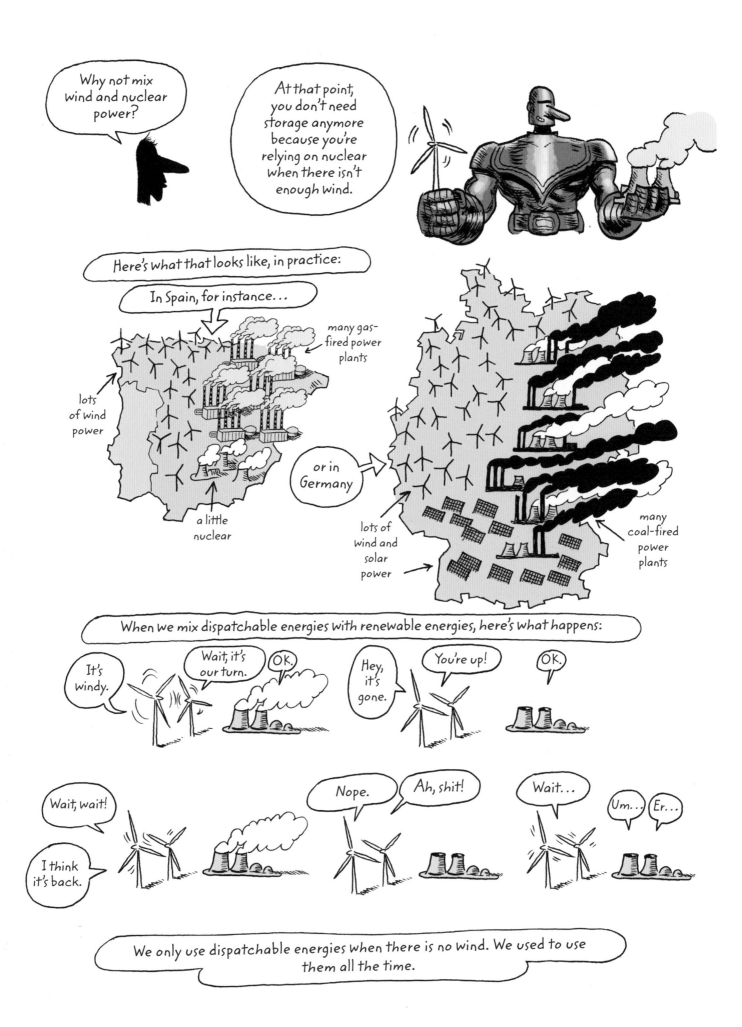

There's a misunderstanding at work. We need to stop thinking that "renewable" means flawless.

Solar paves right over vast tracts of land.

Hydropower floods areas that can be quite sizable and disrupts riparian ecosystems.

Wind power requires a lot of space, degrades agricultural soils, and disturbs the lives of certain species, such as bats.

A lot of metal goes into building wind and solar.

We can use biomass, but only at the expense of ecosystems (remember, it was coal that saved the forests back in 1850).

Sorry, biodiversity!

Forgive the green-house gases!

When you consult the scientists in charge of biodiversity, they point out that there is often a conflict of interest when a new wind or solar project is rolled out.

We do not want renewable energies to be developed at the expense of biodiversity.

Not recommended.

One can hardly accuse this committee's members of being part of a pro-nuclear conspiracy, since until very recently, the Ministry was dead-set against nuclear power.

With 8 billion people and the energy we use...

You have to pick your drawbacks.

NUCLEAR · CO₂ · SURFACE AREA · THREAT TO BIODIVERSITY · CONSUMPTION OF METALS

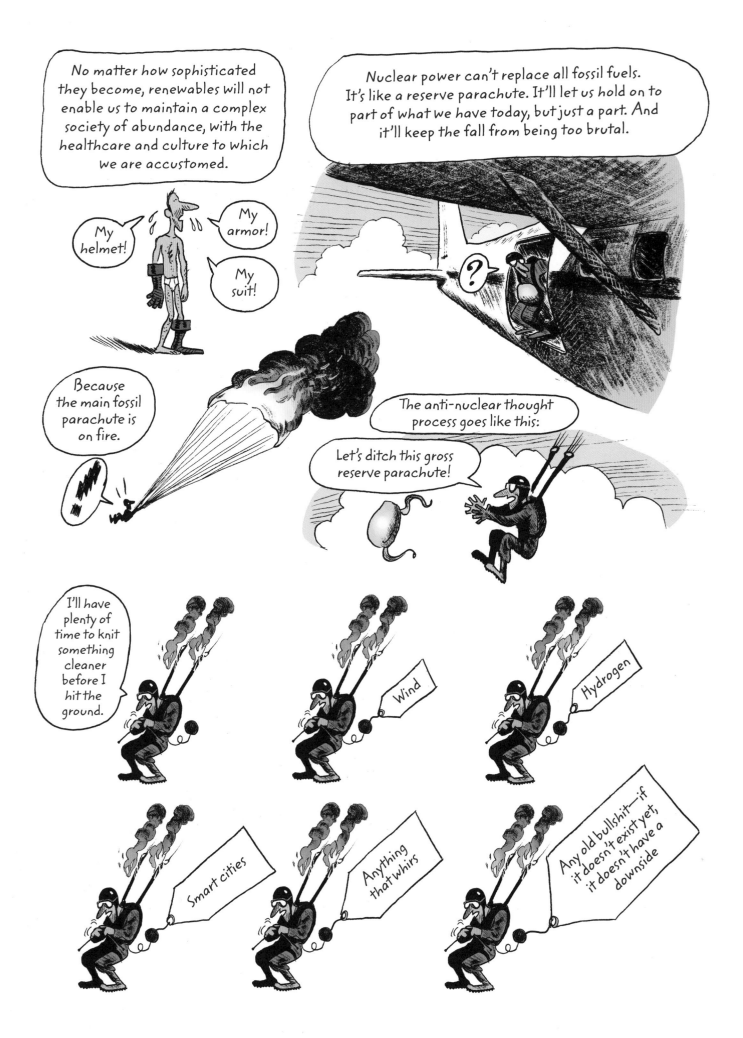

165

Just... less.

It's all about quantity.

The average Westerner should consume 1/2 to 2/3 less meat and dairy products.

Most of which are in processed foods.

You should eat less processed, higher-quality foods in smaller quantities.

Cheese with certified agricultural authenticity

Humanely raised cows fed pesticide-free grass

Remember, the cost of food grew 30 times cheaper over the last 2 centuries.

Tender beef that isn't packed with antibiotics.

You can consume less, better, and on the same budget.

It's not like food is divided into 2 categories...

"Clean" foods you can have as much of as you want...

...and foods that are forbidden no matter what.

The climate problem is a matter of quantity.

The solution is also a matter of quantity.

On the other hand, if we eat less meat and dairy, farmers are going to feel it.

 You can only do so much as an individual.

Beyond that, it's about societal organization.

It's all very well to eat clean...

But what about us?

Our herds are dwindling while restrictions on how we produce only increase.

Society must guarantee them a commensurate increase in income per cow.

In France, this has already been done with AOC—that is, certified agricultural authenticity. Farmers meet specifications and, in exchange, are better paid.

 Not any old livestock!

 Sounds real nice and all, but I've got loans.

So I can produce more!

 Here's a possibility:

 The community shoulders the debt...

...in exchange for a quick, verified conversion.

 Why should the community help private companies overcome their own difficulties?

That's what the US did in the subprime mortgage crisis.

 We need to go organic...

 'Organic' is just another label...

It doesn't address all the challenges facing agriculture. For instance, soil erosion due to overplowing, droughts, and heavy rains...

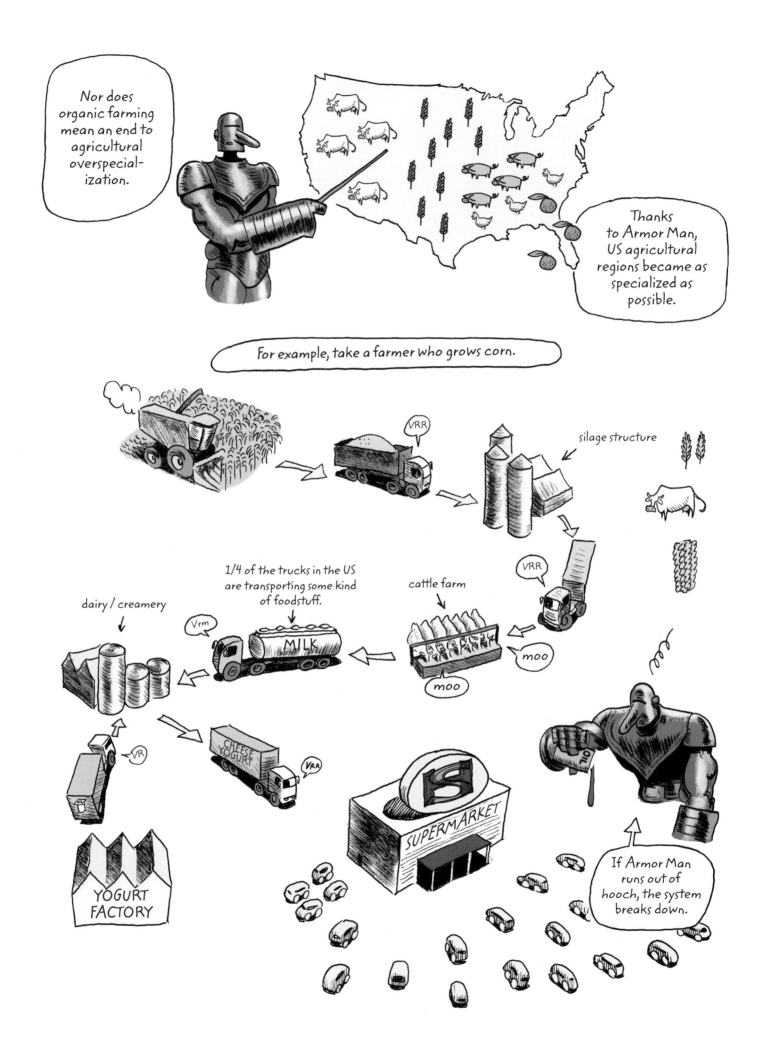

We need to relocalize agriculture to make the system more resilient.

Cows grazing

Chickens eating local wheat

Farmers making their own cheese and yogurt

Truck farming

Pigs eating corn and leftovers

Sort of like our set-up before we used oil for everything. It's more sober as energy use goes.

We're light-years away from this.

This is how American agriculture was organized before the arrival of oil.

We should also avoid gambling on crops or trees that are going to have trouble in a changing climate.

How long would such a change take?

Things change fast when you change farmers.

A farmer retires between 65 and 70. Each new farmer can take things in a new direction.

It takes a little time, about 30 years... But it's not beyond imagining.

Planning a road trip?
Consider getting there by train...

When it comes to long distances,
planes have no competition.

Not flying means giving up travelling
to far away places.

Plenty of business trips can be eliminated
without making much of a difference.

Five percent of the population does half the
air travel. These are people who fly a lot.

Distances mean a change of scenery.
Or they did, early on in commercial aviation.

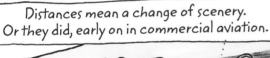

Now most travel is just getting
from one city to another.

Globalization has standardized cities.
Where's the change of scenery?

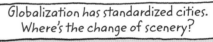

Air travel now means less of a change of scene than it
used to. It's more transportation than travel. Tourism has
become to travel what McDonald's is to food.

1991: 1 billion passengers

2017: 4 billion passengers

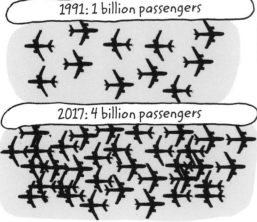

Can we
make
hydrogen
planes?

We already have:
the SLS NASA rocket.

FUEL TANK

4 or 5
passengers

OK, OK!

I get it.

What if you have a family and you're lugging a bunch of stuff?

Why, luggage transport services!

You can also rent a small car upon arrival. All this will cost you less than owning a car year-round.

Highway is my home ♫

And if you really need a car for everyday life, it usually doesn't have to be big or run on gasoline.

A little organization will solve any problem.

What's at stake is preserving peace.

C'mon, everybody pedal!

Cars on the road for vacation have an average occupancy rate of 2.8 people.

Hmm

In daily life, the occupancy rate goes down to 1.1.

People are alone in their cars going to work.

In this case, individuals can make a difference.

telecommuting

carpooling

bicycle (increasingly electric)

buses

trains

When available!

How you combine these means of transportation depends on where you live. Not everyone can give up their cars tomorrow morning. Change isn't equally easy for everyone.

In rural areas with very little public transport, the most efficient, simple, and cheapest low-carbon choice is a small electric car.

Vzzzz

Are electric cars really green? Even with the batteries?

In this case, yes. If they're small.

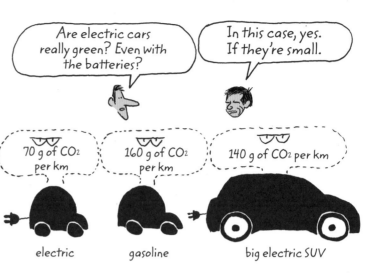

70 g of CO_2 per km

160 g of CO_2 per km

140 g of CO_2 per km

electric

gasoline

big electric SUV

Taking into account emissions from making them and producing electricity in France.

In a country where electricity is more carbon-heavy (e.g., Germany), it looks like this:

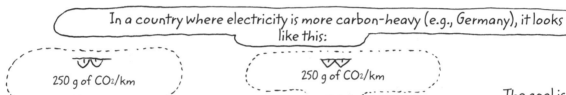

250 g of CO_2/km

250 g of CO_2/km

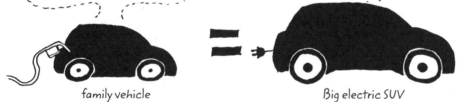

family vehicle

Big electric SUV

The goal is to reduce emissions by 3/4. With small electric cars, you reduce them by 2/3.

At the other end, you have dense cities.

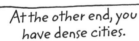

The best thing is walking. In European cities walking has been on the rise since COVID.

It's easy to live car-free there.

↑ bikes, too

← bus, subway…

Electric bikes are a super-efficient solution for replacing cars. They're very easy to use, even if you've got a bald spot and a beer belly. You don't need to be remotely in shape.

Ha ha.

Sure, they require batteries, but the green benefits remain enormous (100x lower emissions than a car).

Electric bikes are an easier step toward redemptive decarbonization than hydrogen cars.

As long as we can still move and get out of our caves, not going as far or as fast won't feel like such a privation.

Getting out is a vital need.

Where are you going?

For some fresh air.

Tell me something else easy I can do?

Here.

RESIDENCIAL & COMMERCAL

13% of US greenhouse gas emissions come from gas or fuel boilers in commerical or residential buildings.

We can insulate homes well.

And use heat pumps.

Heat pumps take cold

or heat

outdoors

or underground

and move it around to heat

or cool (they work as air conditioners)

They're 3 times more efficient than your usual radiator.

They operate on the same principle as a refrigerator.

Don't they emit powerful greenhouse gases?

Sometimes the refrigerants they contain do.

With proper maintenance and care in manufacturing and recycling, these emissions will have a very limited impact.

It sure does sound easy.

Society can provide financial incentives to replace gas and oil boilers.

In France, nuclear production should be increased by 20%.

Heat 'em up!

And/or electricity must be saved by using more efficient appliances in greater moderation...

For instance:

Heads up!

Or low-energy lighting.

Not even hot!

LED

We know how to do that. This alone can save us 7-10%.

There are easy ways to use less electricity. The choice is between nuclear power and consuming less. Either way, we win on emissions and we can organize things to win on job creation, too.

Manufacturing and maintaining heat pumps and power plants domestically reduces gas and oil imports. It also creates jobs.

It makes degrowth palatable.

But wait... With changes in housing, transportation, and possible gains on CO_2 emissions, nuclear is more than a reserve parachute.

It's a *big* reserve parachute.

We retain more freedom of movement.

Here's another, far more difficult one to achieve: land management.

Take suburban shopping malls, with their big box stores.

In a more energy-sober world, will we need such places where people flock by car to buy things they'll soon throw away?

Do we keep some, or get rid of them entirely?

In a broader sense, land-use planning must be reconceived in a world with scarcer energy resources.

Whoa there! Sure that's a good spot for the building?

If we have less transportation and less material flow?

"Grand Paris": a perfect example of a project a century too late.*

* Métropole du Grand Paris: a metropolitan area comprising Paris and the surrounding suburbs, created in 2016 with the aim of fostering sustainable urban, social, and economic development.

Less material flow?

The production of manufactured goods represents 25% of our carbon footprint.

That's a ton!

That's a ton.

CONSUMPTION

STUFF

MORE STUFF

ALL SORTS OF STUFF

SO LONG, fun stuff to buy!

It's not all or nothing. As usual, it's just...

A matter of quantity.

How do I choose?

This or that?

Will you really be happier?

Quit Jiminy-Cricketing me, Jean-Marc!

It drives me nuts!

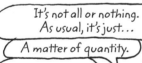

OK already! I get it.

We'll have to buy fewer things, use them for longer, know how to fix them...

Fight against programmed obsolescence, demand longer warranties, create jobs for craftsmen who repair things.

Mm-hm.

Ta-daa!

I give in every now and then...

And chow down on a good veal stew!

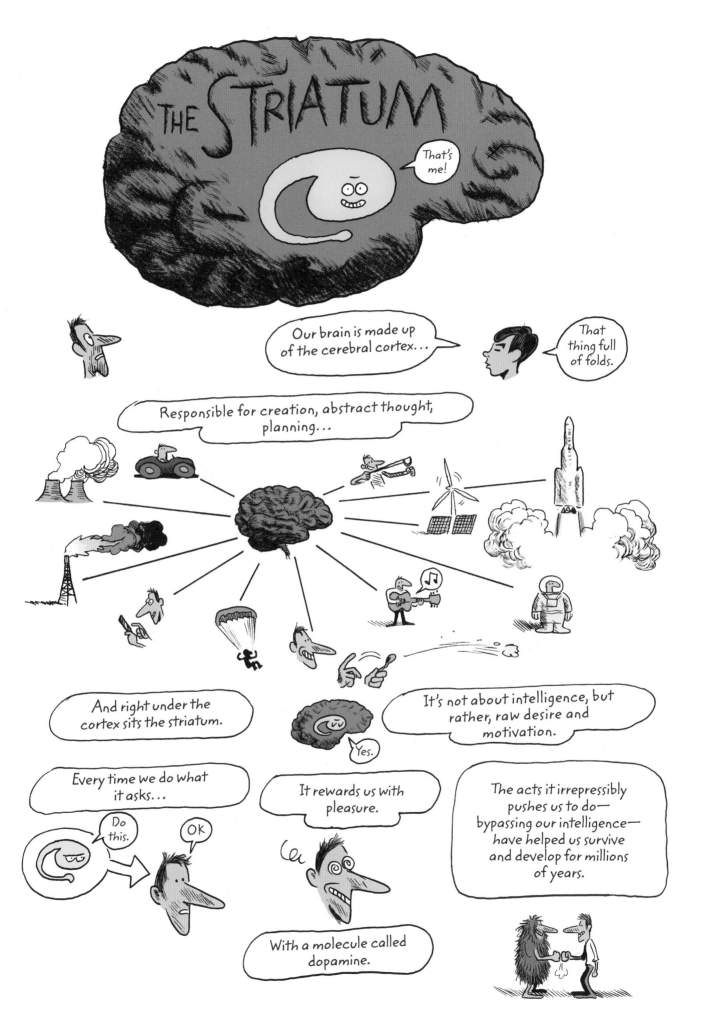

The first of these acts is *eating*.

Once the meal's ready, you'll have to eat fast.

'Cause there's no fridge for leftovers.

And other predators or rivals are on the prowl.

Who knows when I'll ever find such a handsome woolly mammoth again?

Those who eat without restraint are those who survive.

Enough already!

Our desire to eat is not designed for self-restraint.

The more we are able to stock up...

...the more doses of dopamine the striatum rewards us with.

That's for short-term survival. For long-term survival, you have to pass on your genes. That's the second act.

Gr

GRUMF
GROMF

Every time we have sex, the striatum rewards us with a shot of dopamine.

Darwin's theory of evolution tells us that, in order to win the great race of natural selection, you must manage to make more copies of your DNA than your neighbor can. In other words, have more sex.

Here again, the striatum, with its reward system, is not designed for self-restraint. Quite the contrary.

The third act the striatum promotes is acquiring social status.

Being the leader can provide a lot of dopamine.

Every time we climb a rung in the social hierarchy, the striatum rewards us.

The rule of all life is to minimize energy expenditure while maximizing input.

To do as little as possible whenever we get the chance...

Dopamiiiiine

Act no. 4: doing @%&# all.

Last but not least, we crave information...

Hmm

Hmm hmm

GRUMF

Correctly interpreting information can be essential to survival.

← Dude whose interpretation was spot-on

The cortex deploys its efforts to meet the striatum's needs.

Hungry!!

Settle down, I'll take care of it.

THEN

baa

THEN

oink

We've moved from a world of scarcity to one of abundance.

The striatum is always pushing us to want more.

The World Health Organization tells us that more people in the world die from obesity than hunger.

136 billion pornographic videos viewed yearly.

2 or 3 SUVs sold every minute.

social status symbol

The quest for social status now extends to the virtual world.

I want 👍

I want ♥

We do all we can to exert the least effort.

We are suffering from information obesity: "infobesity." Our striata are prey to the slightest alert, the slightest notification, unable to resist.

I'd like to focus just a little, pleeease!

NO!

Scroll up, scroll down! CLICK! CLICK! CLICK!

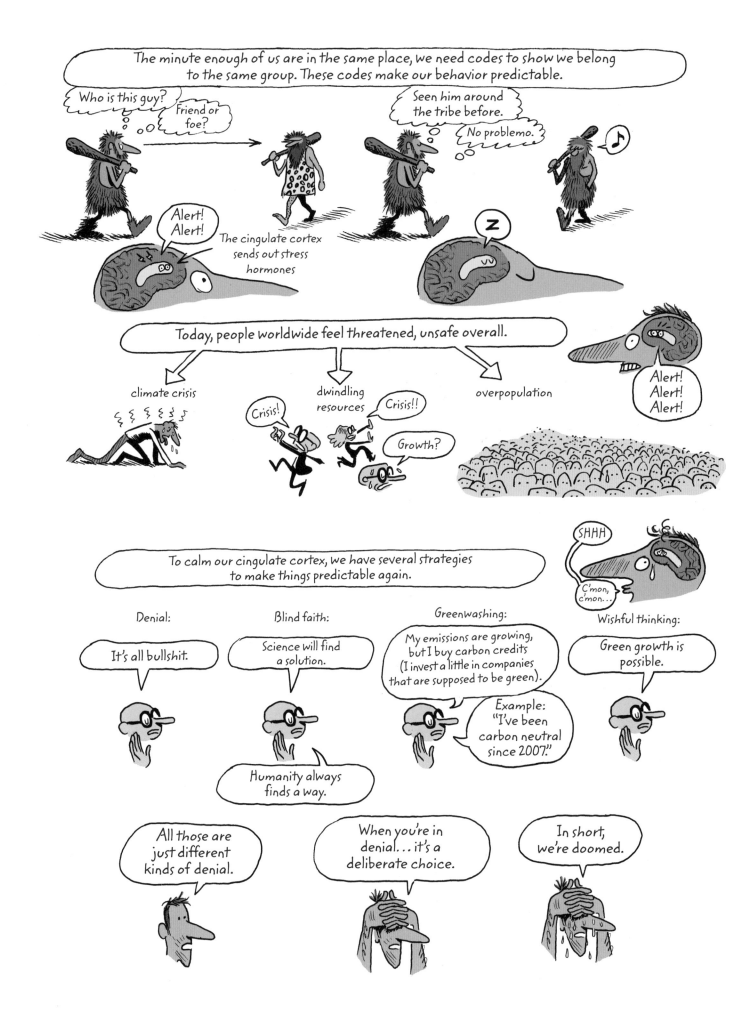

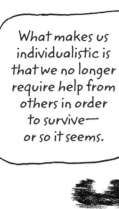

What makes us individualistic is that we no longer require help from others in order to survive— or so it seems.

Your consumer behavior frees you from cooperating.

It all becomes so easy.

If technology can no longer ensure our safety, we must find it in mutual aid.

Resilience isn't about relying solely on your own strengths, but rather creating a network.

You get it now.

Good-bye!

TCHROUF

Sébastien?

We know the old system won't work for much longer.

We must believe and take steps toward things that have a chance of coming true...

Face the problems together and agree on the ways and means.

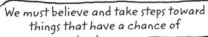

You mean we should all agree with you, and then we'll be saved?

That's usually what people mean when they say we have to get on the same page.

Hahaha!

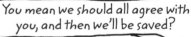

Do you think our brains are as discretely compartmentalized as Sébastien says?

I don't know. But he's basically right about our behavior. I see it in action every day.

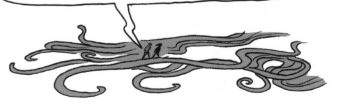

Jean-Marc Jancovici & Christophe Blain December 2023

PARTICULAR BOOKS

UK I USA I Canada I Ireland I Australia
India I New Zealand I South Africa

Particular Books is part of the Penguin Random House group of companies
whose addresses can be found at global.penguinrandomhouse.com.

First published in France as *Le monde sans fin* by DARGAUD 2021
First published in Great Britain by Particular Books 2024
002

The authors wish to extend their thanks and gratitude to Sébastien Bohler for his collaboration.

Christophe Blain would like to thank the Dargaud studio, and Adrien Samson in particular,
for their assistance in finalizing this book.

Jean-Marc Jancovici would like to thank Christophe Blain for his trust and confidence.
Colourists: Clémance Sapin and Christophe Blain

Translated by Edward Gauvin
Printed in Italy by Printer Trento SrL

The authorized representative in the EEA is Penguin Random House Ireland,
Morrison Chambers, 32 Nassau Street, Dublin D02 YH68

A CIP catalogue record for this book is available from the British Library

ISBN: 978-0-241-66194-9

www.greenpenguin.co.uk